PIONEER JOURNAL: A Modern-Day Journey to an Unknown World

Golden Heart Publications
PO BOX 6759
Santa Fe, NM, 87502

This book is based on real-life experiences. Some names have been changed to insure privacy.

The front cover art was painted by Russell Lawson, Seattle, Washington.
Edited by Brandt Morgan, Santa Fe, New Mexico

The back cover photo was taken in September, 1993 in Galisteo, New Mexico, as the four of us worked in "Wyatt Earp" starring Kevin Costner and directed by Lawrence Kasdan.

ISBN 0-9634920-3-9

Library of Congress Catalog Card Number: 94-75295
Hall, Michael
Pioneer Journal: A Modern-Day Journey to an Unknown World
First Printing, 1994
Non-fiction
Religion
New Age

In honor of our connection with them, many of the quotes at the beginning of each chapter are from actual diaries of pioneers who crossed the American continent during the 1850s. I am grateful to Lillian Schlissel, author of Women's Diaries of the Westward Journey and co-author of Far From Home, for the thousands of hours she labored to compile them.

Printed in the United States of America, on recycled paper, with soy ink.
This book was printed by Griffin Printing, Sacramento California.
Griffin is one of the few book printers in the U.S. which uses recycled paper as its standard stock. I am grateful to Penny Hancock and the entire staff there for their help and support.

PIONEER JOURNAL
A Modern-Day Journey
to an Unknown World

Michael Hall

ACKNOWLEDGMENTS

- I acknowledge the pain of all who have ever seen friends leave their world.
- I acknowledge those who, despite that pain, gave unconditional love and support to those who left.
- I acknowledge those who made the journey before us, and who, immediately upon our arrival in the new world, became old friends.
- My wife, Annie, woman of great strength and spirit, for being a pioneer in her own right.
- Bob, Rick, and Nancy, for loving a changing brother.
- Dr. Judy Scher, for honoring this pioneer with each baby step taken toward living in his body.
- Robin Ann Hunter and David Conrey, for serving as loving way-showers to Santa Fe and beyond.
- Butch and Cheryl Tongate, for proof-reading, Reiki, and for Adrienne, Allison, and A.J.
- Judy and John Graham, for editing, and for their impeccability.
- Walter Krokowski, who, by sharing his gifts, made the publication of this book possible.
- Kate Hall, and Andrew Hall, my incredible children, for choosing this wild ride of life with Annie and Mike Hall. "Are you *still* working on Pioneer Journal, Daddy?"

I dedicate this journal to

my mother, June, and my father, Bob,

and to

Annie's mother, Clare, and her father, George . . .

who watched their children move
toward the edge of an abyss
wider and deeper
and more formidable
than the Grand Canyon itself.

My wish and disclosed motive, as I made plans to share my "pioneer's journal" with the public, was that it serve not as one person's tale of the "other side," but as a crude map of one path toward awakening, such as the early mountain men left for the first settlers.

—Pioneer Journal

PREFACE

When my editor, Brandt Morgan, first read the manuscript for this book, he said, "I was confused. I kept wondering when the journey would begin. Then I realized that your 'journey' took two years. You need to tell your readers that this is not just about a trip from New York to the West."

So here goes: This is not a book about a trip from New York to the West. I use the term "journey" throughout this book in the broadest sense, for, unlike the hardy pioneers of the 1800s, the trip to the Southwest from New York takes either six hours (including the stopover in Chicago) or three days (the way Annie and I drive our motor home!)

During the two years encompassed by this story, we took *three* trips to the Southwest, all while crossing mountains of uncertainty and pushing into the headwind of disapproval. And even more difficult than a several thousand mile drive or angry family member were the constant inner arguments about whether and why we should make such a move, and whether or not I was crazy.

Add to the mix the fact that we left neither famine nor flood; even in the midst of the recession of the late eighties and early nineties, I was still earning a hundred thousand dollars a year. After Annie and I sold our big home and paid off our debts—a story I tell in *Flight Lessons,* that was a lot of income. To make the status quo still more attractive, I had earned that much working only ten to twenty hours a *week.*

Ten hours a week and lots of money. Perfect for a man who loved to be home with his children. Dreamlike for an aspiring writer. We could hop into our twenty-seven foot motor home almost at will and head for Florida, Montana, Canada, or New Mexico. We lived in a large house on two lush, landscaped acres that cost us a fourth of what the house we sold had cost. We lived in a great little school district and were surrounded by friends. Incredible lifestyle. The American Dream. Perfect. Friends and family to this day continue to scratch their heads and say, "Whatever happened to Mike Hall?" But we HAD TO GO.

It took us two years and three scouting trips, during which we explored forty states and thirty thousand miles of America's highways. Seven hundred thirty long days and sleepless nights from when we decided to move to the Southwest until we landed there. During that time, I carried my journals with me day and night. The six hundred pages of those journals and the two hundred fifty pages you are about to read reveal only small parts of those days.

Such was our journey. This book tells the story of those scouting trips, the confusion, and the many wonderful and strange experiences that followed the commitment Annie and I made to "seize the day," to build our new life, and to follow our dreams. If at times the story seems tedious, it is because that's how the *journey* often was.

Santa Fe, New Mexico
June, 1994

~~~

The italicized sections of this book come, word for word, from my journals.

ONE

Our discontent and restlessness were enhanced by the fact that my health was not good. The physician advised an entire change of climate . . . and finally approved of our contemplated trip across the plains in a "Prairie schooner." In any case, as in that of many others, my health was restored long before the end of our journey.
—From the diary of Catherine Haun, 1849

THE TUG OF RESTLESSNESS

This pioneer journal started as a 1990s tale that would parallel the journeys of the brave pioneers of the early and mid-nineteenth century. Those early pioneers crossed the wild and unpaved American continent by wagon, horse, and foot. Our "prairie schooner" would be a 1991 motor home with three hundred horses under the hood, a hot shower, a stove, a microwave, and a color TV with a VCR.

I soon started to question this. The parallel of our journeys with the journeys of the early pioneers, many of whom buried more than one family member along on the side of the trail, was less than cute. Some of those 1850s travelers died or experienced horrors like scalpings, being skinned alive, or even a fellow pioneer's report that their children had become his food supply ("The ox was too dry," the survivor said) in Donner Pass.

Why did those early pioneers make the trip? Why did *we*? There lay the true comparison. Like Catherine Haun, my health was not good either. My heart and chest hurt every day I practiced law. Like her, my health was restored long before journey's end. And, like her, a constant feeling of discontent and restlessness made an illogical, impractical, and imprudent journey inevitable. My pioneer journal was a chronicle of the restlessness that had driven me since birth.

~~~

Restlessness. "Leave well enough alone!" my parents had yelled after I switched the seat on my bicycle two days after I got it for my birthday. They had repeated the phrase every time I tried to fix a working radio or make better what everyone else thought was fine.

I'm sure they also thought it, but bit their tongues, when their seven-year-old son, Michael John cut off his finger while "fixing" the lawn mower.

As my teen years approached, the restlessness grew. I shared a few of these stories in *Flight Lessons*, but there were too many to write about. After my days of model airplane building had passed, I read road maps and sketched the camper I would build on top of my 1957 Chevy pickup. I bought that truck for a hundred twenty-five dollars on my sixteenth birthday and took it on dozens of backpacking and ski adventures all around New England. I wanted to do even more.

The following summer my friend Jack Wrightington and I crammed two backpacks and a tent into the back of his fresh-off-the-lot green Chevy Vega station wagon and tied two bikes to the roof. Five weeks later, the odometer read eleven thousand and a huge world had filled my eyes and imagination.

We backpacked deep into the wilderness of Glacier National Park, where I quivered in our little nylon tent as I heard grizzlies nearby tearing through packs in the night. I galloped on a chestnut mare across a yellow-and-gold alpine meadow in the Canadian Rockies, swam in the icy Pacific, and spoke some of the Spanish Jack had taught me in a tiny town in Mexico.

But I was restless, and such adventures never quench a restless one's thirst for more. Between the time I received my junior driver's license on my sixteenth birthday and my high school graduation, I drove almost a hundred thousand miles, which included three round trips to Salt Lake City and a hundred backpacking expeditions from Maine to Tennessee.

When I first met Annie, she talked about living in the mountains, and I shared with her my never-ending love for travel. But except for a business trip to Chicago, somehow our mountains had become our growing careers and ever bigger houses. Our travels were nothing more than rushed commutes to real estate closings.

But nothing, not distractions or antagonistic voices, can kill dreams. Just before the ten years in the fast lane of the 1980s drained the spirit from us, the old restlessness returned. For everyone around us, our lives had exceeded the American Dream. We had two beautiful children, a house on the water, and a six-figure income. But I could not leave well enough alone.

It was around that time that the visions came. I often saw pictures. It was in the late 1980s, during dreams or contemplations or at random times in the day, that I started seeing a house in a desert setting. The setting was what I imagined Arizona might look like. Dreams of that house, or just faint messages about the Southwest from who-knows-where, found their way into my journal.

Yet even in *my* adventurous mind, such a vision made little sense. In those hundred thousand miles and during my trip with Jack, I visited thirty states, but Arizona was not one of them. In my mind, New Mexico did not even exist...until the visions showed up.

Annie and I heeded the call. In 1989, we left Kate and Andrew, then one and three, with Grandma and Grandpa Murray, and flew to Arizona. As we scooted around Sedona in our little rental car, I actually looked for the house in my visions the way Natalie Wood looked for her dream house in *Miracle on Thirty-Fourth Street*. I never found the house. We both fell in love with the Southwest nevertheless. Even back then, we knew it was time to move West.

I guess that is where the journey of the pioneers of the 1990s began: with a seed planted in a restless soul, then nurtured and fed by a Spirit more powerful than wind, criticism, doubts, or even fire and water.

Two weeks after that first short trip to Arizona, our house in New York was under contract and we had started shopping for a motor home. We dreamed of traveling the continent with our two children and scoping out the country for a new home. Then, like the pioneers who crossed this country in the early 1800s, we would pack up our belongings and head West!

TWO

Sell your farm . . . and come to this valley; don't stay in that inhospitable climate. I would rather eat off a tin plate and live in a tent in California than have the best house and farm in Illinois.

— Excerpt of a letter to Roxana Cheney Foster from her father-in-law, 1852.

CRAZY

"What the heck are they doing there?" I asked myself.

Four of them, standing beside a shack. No, not a shack. A hut. Even less. A pile of sod clumps leaning in the middle of a barren field with a little opening on one side. A mustachioed, soiled man in worn boots, tattered shirt, and stitched pants stands before this mud pile. A woman stands beside him, wiping sweat and dirt from her sullied face. Flickers of light shine from the eyes of two children with mud-black faces and ragged clothes. Somehow, though, this family stands upright and tall. All four faces say, "This is our home."

I first met that pioneer family when they appeared on the pages of my grade school history book. The caption under the picture read "Homesteaders, 1863." They were the true pioneers of the mid-nineteenth century, the daring and the hopeful that risked their lives to follow their dreams.

In fourth grade music, Mr. Beebe taught us, "Oh don't you remember sweet Betsy from Pike, who crossed o'er the mountains with her husband Ike?" Two yoke of oxen. A big yellow dog. I could not see the dirt on sweet Betsy's face. I never imagined Ike and Betsy winding up in a mud hut in the middle of nowhere.

How did they get there? How did they survive the trek across America's vastness without maps or roads? Without AAA or rest stops or Howard Johnsons? And who did they leave behind? And why? What the heck did they go there for? The history books talked about things like "escaping religious persecution," the "Manifest Destiny" and such, but the faces in the picture did not say "We're free." They did not say, "We enlarged America." They said, "We're here. We *did* it!"

Despite the grade school songs and myopic views of textbooks, I wondered why anyone would leave the relative comforts of the East Coast —lush, green trees, clear, running rivers, temperate climate, and fertile soil—for the wild, barren, dry, and dusty territories like Oklahoma or New Mexico. It was crazy.

~~~

January 26, 1992
Southold, New York

"Are you crazy?" my father yelled. "What are you running away from? What are you going to do there?"

"Nothing." I said, taking a perch on top of my desk so I didn't feel so small, trying to act more defenseless than I felt. "I just don't belong here. And you know I don't want to be a lawyer anymore."

Seven o'clock in the morning was the only time even a little bit of peace touched my law office. By eight, three phones would be ringing. By nine, my secretary (it had been three secretaries before I started scaling down the practice) would be keeping two of those lines on hold while asking me for instructions.

At seven, before the hyper pace and frantic feelings began to take over, I would nervously prepare the day's work while Dad nursed his coffee, scraped the excess butter off his roll, and started the New York Times crossword puzzle. After the small talk ("How's my little Kate and Andy?"), new jokes and old wisdom were the order of the day. We had practiced together for almost ten years, and I never would have guessed that my announcement would shock him.

"But you have it so good," he said. Then he listed how "good" I had it, "Who else do you know that makes a hundred thousand bucks a year and still has the free time you have? You're your own boss, you can come and go as you please. You and Annie and the kids have your motor home and can travel as much as you want. You own this office and live in this beautiful place."

Then his list changed, and his voice rose higher still. "What are you going to the damn desert for? It took man thousands of years to get out of the stupid desert. What the hell do you think you're gonna do there?"

Maybe five times in my life had I seen my father that angry. Maybe. As my brothers and sisters and I grew up, he had always shown a positive attitude and worn a "life is great" face. He had always said, "In fifty years, nobody will ever know the difference." Always. Yet something in his voice that day told me that my plans *had* made a difference. All tolerance seemed to have deserted him.

I expected Dad to be excited about Annie and me moving to New Mexico. When I had decided to attended a college two thousand miles from home, Dad had given me unconditional support and showed only excitement.

Yet there I sat on my oak desk in my own law office, caught off guard by what felt like a sudden recurrence of the Inquisition. I imagined an imposing figure in black robes saying, "So you want to leave the Church, do you?" as he poured lye into a heretic's eyes or sentenced him to rot in a rat-filled prison.

Dad's church wasn't the fact that his "number three son" was a successful attorney. Dad's church was Logic, and my intention to move was obviously illogical. I couldn't blame him, really; since it was illogical to me, it must have been really crazy to him. I had just told him I intended to give up a practice in which I was earning what he saw as easy money. I had just told him that Annie and I and his two grandchildren were leaving the bucolic seaside town of Southold, New York, the place he considered the most beautiful on earth. I might as well have just told a fifteenth-century monk that the earth was round, that it was not the center of the universe.

There remained one last question: "What are you going to *do* there?"

"I don't know what I'm going to do, Dad," I said. "Annie and I want to move West, and I have to get out of this business."

"Michael John, Michael John," he muttered, shaking his head. "You were always the sensible one. How are you going to live? Everyone has to make a living."

"We're in pretty good shape now. We've sold the big house and are renting. That alone is saving us two thousand bucks a month. When we get out West, I'll stay home with the kids and work on my writing. Annie will probably work as an addictions counselor."

"So you're going to live on fifteen thousand dollars a year?"

"Dad, if I have to wait tables, I will. I just can't do this anymore."

~~~

January 29, 1992
Southold

A few days after the confrontation with my father, some cousins came to visit us in our rented house. The whole family sat in the kitchen. We were all making small talk, but Annie could not wait. "We're moving to New Mexico in June," she said. "Right after Katie's last day of Kindergarten."

No response. Silence. Perhaps they were not surprised because Annie and I had talked incessantly about the West and about moving there for much of the past year. Maybe they expected it, but the silence was heavy with tension.

"What are you running away from?"one of the cousins asked Annie. Then another turned to her. "How can you leave your family?" The questions, like my father's, felt more accusatory than inquisitive.

"*This* is my family," she replied, motioning to Andrew, Kate, and me. Annie was never hesitant about talking things out with family, hers or mine. Despite all the hostility and anger that stared us down for the second time in a week, Annie stood steadfast.

"But why do you have to go so far?" her cousin demanded. As I heard the question, I remembered a young couple I had represented that week. "My mother is horrified that we have moved so far," the woman told me. They had purchased a home *forty miles* from their native Queens, New York.

"We'll only be a plane ride away," Annie said. More silence.

"You need a home. You have children." These declarations didn't even pretend to be questions.

"We're home wherever we are," Annie retorted with cool poise. "It doesn't depend on what kind of house we're in, or even if we're in a house."

Then one of our guests, unknowingly repeating something another relative had said to me earlier that week, said, "Since you were young, you've never been satisfied."

Neither Annie nor I replied. She was right.

~~~

"Our families feel abandoned." Annie said that night as we lay in bed. "They're not really angry." She propped up her pillows and snuggled next to me.

I thought of the incredible things that Annie and I had experienced in the year since we had begun our travels. The adventures would have to had been seen to be believed. "If only we could tell them about what happened in Sedona," I said.

Sedona?" Annie said. "What about Santa Fe, and Minnesota, and British Columbia?

"Yeah, and Jackson, Wyoming, and Phoenicia," I said, recalling the innocent stops along our journeys that had brought profound experiences.

"But we can't tell them, Michael. They would all think we're crazy."

"They already think we're crazy, Annie," I said. "Anyway, they'll understand more when they read the book."

As this conversation took place in January of 1992, my first book, *Flight Lessons*, sat on a senior editor's desk a hundred miles away in New York City. Though I knew some of the stores in that book would help our families understand us a little better, I also knew it could take a year to get it out in print.

"But *Flight Lessons ends* in Sedona, doesn't it?" Annie asked. I nodded affirmatively. Then she said, "Most of the really way-out things happened after that. They still won't understand."

She was right. The two-year odyssey into a world more strange and illogical than we ever imagined had begun one day in the winter of 1991, when we packed Kate and Andrew (then just four and two), a month's worth of food, and my journal into our 1991 TravelMaster motor home. That day we started the second of three scouting trips into pioneer country, into the American Southwest.

~~~

THREE

Travel is fatal to prejudice, bigotry and narrow-mindedness, and many of our people need it sorely.
. . . Broad, wholesome, charitable views . . . can not be acquired by vegetating in one's little corner of Earth.
— Mark Twain, *Innocents Abroad*

FROM SEA LEVEL TO SPACE, AND HIGHER

January, 1991

We pulled out of our driveway at about six in the evening. The first hour took us past the potato farms and vineyards of Eastern Long Island and to the beginning of the Long Island Expressway. An hour and a half after that we crossed from Long Island to the mainland on the Throgs Neck Bridge, and we headed down the Cross Bronx Expressway toward the George Washington Bridge.

The ten miles across the Bronx were tougher than ten thousand would be anywhere else in the U.S. Potholes rattled the motor home to the point where I thought the overhead cabinets would tumble down on Kate and Andrew. Carcasses of cars, left by roving gangs who strip them down to the frame in a matter of minutes, dotted the roadside. Graffiti on the trains overhead matched the spray-painted thirty-foot walls into which this highway was sunk, making the road look and feel like a Valley of Death.

At that moment, I did not see that ghastly gauntlet as a symbol of what we would have to go through in order to really leave behind the American Dream. I just clutched the wheel and counted down the minutes until we would be out of that horrible city. Eighteen hours later, at a rest stop which would serve as our camp for the night, I had time to grab my diary and log something less intense and perhaps more important than the Valley of Death:

January 20, 1991 11:30 P.M.
Memphis, Tennessee

As we cruised a hilly, green pothole-free Interstate 40, Kate asked me, "Are there snakes in Texas?"
"Yes," I told her, "but not in the winter."
"Do they go south like birds do?"

The earlier pioneers on the Santa Fe or Oregon Trails covered fifteen miles on a good day. That first day we drove seven hundred miles. After you've been buzzing along at sixty-five miles an hour for eighteen hours, your body keeps on buzzing after you stop. Inner bodies move. They also remember.

Four days later, we had settled into the American RV Park ten miles west of Albuquerque. Shortly after the sun rose over Sandia Peak, we put candles in a chocolate frosted doughnut and sang "Happy Birthday" to Andrew. Andrew's smile mirrored my joy as he celebrated his third birthday. From his point of view, high on his Fisher Price child seat, huddled in the motor home's dinette between his mom and dad and sister, Andrew was not two thousand miles from home. He was home.

During the following week, we stayed in Santa Fe in the driveway of our friend Robin Ann Hunter. Robin Ann was also a student of Eckankar, sometimes known as the religion of the light and sound of God. One night we attended an Eckankar HU chant together, where several people gathered to sing the holy word, HU. A chance encounter there with a woman named Nancy jolted me. I shared with her my dream of being on TV with Phil Donahue and Oprah. Something about her way of listening energized me. I told her how important it felt to me to share my story with the world.

She stopped me, then gently grasped my shoulder. With warm eyes and a ring of wisdom and strength I will never forget, she pointed to Kate and Andrew playing on the floor of her home. "Those are the most important things in the whole universe," she said. "Take care of them—give them attention and love— and you may indeed change the world."

February 2, 1991
Albuquerque, New Mexico

Freedom
Responsibility
"Listen. We are all. Free. To do. Whatever. We want. To do."
That's what Donald Shimoda told Richard Bach in Illusions.
For 35 years, I have done what I wanted—as long as it was OK with my father-mother-boss-wife-teacher . . .
Freedom—the balloon.
Responsibility — the ballast.

A little ballast makes smooth and controlled the flight of freedom, protecting me from a too-rapid rise to the sun or a smash against the rocks.

I wrote that entry after flying in a hot air balloon high over a beautiful, over that new yet ancient place called New Mexico. That balloon flight was the culmination of life-long dreams for both Annie and me. But perhaps due to that reminder from Nancy, I wrote of ballast, of freedom, and of responsibility. Some months later, it would strike me that in my hundred-odd viewings of *The Wizard of Oz*, I had identified with Dorothy's journeys to another world, yet had forgotten that the Omaha State Fair balloon was to take the wizard and Dorothy not over the rainbow but *home*. The journey to "far away" is the journey home. From that pinnacle, we moved on.

~~~

With our hair still sticky and wet with cheap champagne (a tradition showered on those who touch ground after their maiden balloon flight), we climbed aboard our TravelMaster and headed towards Sedona, Arizona. Sedona is the land where the Mogollon Rim drops from Flagstaff's seven thousand feet to four thousand, and where I sometimes felt like the red rocks were singing ancient songs.

Sedona is a red rocked, green-treed fairy land. Other than a few dreams, which I had logged with discipline, this is what I wrote after three days there:

Remember, Mike, about:

Living in this moment (Spirit is working in your life; the changes are natural steps)

Love (for family, friends, Life)

Gratitude (for all the help and support)

Compassion (for those in pain)

Honesty (to yourself, to Annie)

Detachment (from archaic laws and thoughts that hold you down)

Dreams (waking and sleeping—nearly direct billboards from Spirit)

Mahanta (that manifestation of Spirit able to work directly with the individual)

Economy (the direct path)

Trust (in God)

Then something wonderful happened: our motor home developed serious engine trouble. It had only eight thousand miles on it. "I wish Honda made a motor home," Annie muttered that day as we chugged from Sedona into Cottonwood at fifteen miles an hour.

"Let's hope they can take us in right away at the Ford dealer," I said to Annie as I pictured us stranded without a car in Cottonwood, Arizona. "Otherwise we'll have to walk to a motel and sit there while they fix it."

Dr. Bernie Siegel, the author of *Love, Medicine, and Miracles*, would have called our car trouble a "spiritual flat tire," for something magical transpired as a result of it. It brought us to a service manager named A.J. at Verde Valley Ford. At eight A.M., I stood at the busy service desk with Annie and our children, visualizing him telling us to come back tomorrow. I explained the symptoms and our predicament.

"I'll have somebody look at it right away," he assured us. "Can you drive a five speed?" His question puzzled me.

"Sure," I said as he walked through a doorway.

A minute later, he returned, holding out a key. "This is for that white Festiva in the parking lot. If you come back at four, we'll have your motor home ready for you." Annie and I looked at each other, wide-eyed with surprise.

"Have you seen the Indian ruins at Tuzigoot?" he asked. He then gave us directions to Tuzigoot and some other sights. We buckled Andrew's child seat into the back of the loaner car, climbed in, and headed toward the mountains.

The four of us walked around the narrow, cliff-side shops of the former ghost town of Jerome. We had lunch in a tiny place called Macy's that was built on a switchback and shaped like a pie slice.

From Jerome, at five thousand feet, we drove up to Prescott National Forest and walked in the tall pine trees at a campsite called Potato Patch. Eight thousand feet up, February 6th, and sixty degrees. The blue sky defined the magic of the day; the pine forest energized me.

We returned with a dozen brownies for A.J and the workers at Verde Valley Ford, then drove back to Sedona.

The day that started with a broken-down motor home in rural Arizona, ended in an ice cream parlor in Sedona. As I sat wiping ice cream off Andrew's chin and onto his lap and nursing my own waffle cone filled with mint chocolate chip, a tall, gray-haired man in light blue sweat pants turned to me. "Always come from the heart. That will get you past your left brain/right brain struggle." Then he walked out.

Annie and I looked at each other and smiled. Were we once again seeing that reminders from Spirit come from many sources, and that spiritual masters wear all kinds of disguises, from automobile service managers to ice cream eaters.

After Kate and Andrew curled up in their twin beds at the rear of the RV that night, Annie told of a reminder she had received earlier in the day. "I got a message from Spirit this morning when we were up in the forest," she said. As we had learned from our studies of Eckankar, messages from Spirit came through many signs around us—from weather patterns to newspaper headlines to dreams.

A year earlier, Annie and I had hiked into one of Sedona's energy vortices, also known as planetary power sites, to contemplate. Contemplation is not about talking to God, it is about listening. That day, as she started her contemplation, Annie had asked Spirit what her next spiritual step was to be. She received a direct answer: "Be ready for anything." Now, in a campground very near to that same spot, she was telling me of another answer from contemplation.

"What was it?"I begged her.

"Santa Fe," she said. Then, without another word, she rolled over and went to sleep.

~~~

February 8, 1991
Sedona

We kept moving, even within a given town. We searched for a better campground within Sedona. As we backed our motor home under a cottonwood tree at the Schnebly Hill Campground, one of the several strange events that never saw the pages of my first book occurred. Even as I wrote about the phenomenal events in *Flight Lessons*, I was not ready to share the story of the woman we met there.

"Hi, I'm Cathy."

"Mike Hall," I replied. Before I even got a chance to shake her hand and meet her husband, Andrew and Kate had Cathy's two dogs barking at them from behind a chaise lounge. Cathy and her husband, Chris, invited Annie and me to see their trailer.

"I thought I was the only nut who carried a computer in my RV," I said. Though we had met not even two minutes before, I somehow felt comfortable enough with her to ask, "What are you working on?"

"Oh," she answered quietly, "I'm writing a book on spirituality."

"Me too," I exclaimed. As I said it I could feel she was not as eager to talk about her work as I.

"What are you guys doing here in Sedona?" she asked, changing the subject.

"We're here to see if we want to live here," Annie said. "We were here last year at this time and really fell in love with it."

We moved outside to chaise lounges and continued the conversation. Under the shade of cottonwood trees, with the magical sound of Oak Creek humming beside us, Annie and I shared our life stories and adventures with this young couple. I drifted in and out of the conversation, lost in the awe of the beyond-Disney setting.

Then, as I sat there watching my young children play at creekside, and my wife talk with a couple whom we would never have met in rural New York, I realized why Mark Twain said, "Travel is fatal to narrow-mindedness."

Much of what I thought was "me," including many opinions and prejudices, would die during our journey into the new. And what of Mark Twain's "broad views?" Before that first motor home trip, I could not have imagined how "broad" broad could become.

The reality we saw as we had traveled would replace the need for imagined things.

~~~

"So what's your book about?" Cathy asked, suddenly ready to talk about something she had shunned just minutes earlier. Maybe because Annie and I were being ourselves, Cathy felt more open with us. But only a few minutes had passed since we had met; maybe there was more to it than that.

I told her about my obsession with flight and my first out-of-body experience as a youth, which in turn led to a life-long spiritual search, and how that in turn led to still more experiences in what I referred to as the "other worlds."

"Oh yeah?" she said. "Then we have similar backgrounds. When I was only ten, I had my first experience with the extraterrestrials. I've been in contact with them ever since."

Annie glanced my way, yet neither she nor I moved so much as an eyebrow. We knew we were on an adventure, but this seemed a bit much. As I looked at Cathy, I thought, *She doesn't seem like a crackpot.* My knowledge of "ETs" was limited to Steven Spielberg's movie by the same name and reruns of *Star Trek*, which I viewed as nothing more than brilliant fiction.

"They communicate with me telepathically," she continued. "I can contact them at will." I sat there with my discriminatory filters up. During my ten years as a lawyer I had learned that some people (even your own clients) can look you in the eye and lie. Then she proceeded to describe to Annie and me how certain focus and intent ("It has to be out of pure love," she said emphatically) brought instantaneous flashes of light in the sky and subsequent direct communication. My wife and I could not say much more than "Oh really?" and "And then what?"

We had left New York two weeks before looking for a new home. What could this bright, seemingly intelligent woman who said she had been in direct communication with beings from other planets have to do with this new home?

By the end of that first afternoon in Sedona, my narrow mindedness about ET phenomena had died. Maybe that is what Twain meant by "fatal." I would find out more as I continued traveling.

~~~

That evening, we attended the opening talk of our first Network Chiropractic Transformational Gate. A Gate is a three-day Network Chiropractic seminar consisting of talks, music, slide presentations, classes, and chiropractic adjustments utilizing the Network spinal analysis method.

At a Gate, fifty to seventy-five people are being adjusted at the same time. The sole purpose of the adjustments, as I understood it, was to "clear the spine of interference" so that the life force can flow more freely. Little did I dream what the flow of that life force could feel like.

Two days later, after a chiropractic adjustment given by Dr. Donald Epstein, I wrote:

February 10, 1991
Sedona, Arizona

I was lying on the table, sobbing.
It was a cry of sheer awe. Awe for the love that had helped bring me to this point. As I lay there bawling, eyes closed, Donald placed a tissue in my outstretched hand. This was the moment, his gift of facilitation, of support, through the most intimate (and universal) threshold, of transformation.

The gratitude and love I felt at that moment became universal. I felt the suffering of those in the room around me. Inwardly, I hugged my brother, then my mother, my father, my wife.

I wept for all those people. Then I remembered: there was someone I had not hugged. Me.

It was me I wept for. Then I embraced myself the way a kind mother embraces a tired baby. I hugged. I held. I loved myself.

I cried for the love I had forgotten to give myself all those eons.

When I embraced myself, something powerful happened— something even more profound than these intense moments of joy, release, discovery, and self-love:

I saw the Altar of God and the Temple of All life. They were literally in me. They were me. When I loved myself so, I realized my worthiness, my inherent holiness. Then I asked with love that the temple doors be opened for me.

And they opened.

Then a new inner knowingness: Before entering the temple doors, all baggage had to be left behind. ALL baggage: Guilt. Personality. Fear. Hesitation. Habits. Religion. All knowledge.

Only the naked heart may enter the temple. Only the naked heart . . .

I entered the temple and approached the altar as neither male nor female.

Even God (my mind's conception of It) had to be left outside. I could only enter the temple alone. I could only approach the altar as an open heart.

The altar glowed and pulsed a brilliant yellow-white light.

~~~

Just two weeks into our first big motor home journey, our "little corner of the earth," as Twain called it, had grown from the little town of Southold, New York, to wondrous places like Santa Fe and Taos, to a magical balloon flight over the Rio Grande River, to other star systems, even to what I saw as the "Altar of God." Where could we possibly go from there?

No plan or place could follow that incredible series of events, so we moved on. We just "went with the flow," a weak expression that was gaining more meaning as each day passed. For that trip, and for most of the year and a half that followed, we lived a life that could not possibly have been planned or put into any kind of itinerary.

From the time we crossed the Hudson River on our voyage to randomness, that pioneer journey, Annie and I left the world of logic behind. In the same way, when the original pioneers left the East Coast, they had intentionally begun a journey into a new world.

But where could we possibly go from the incredible heights of awareness and awe we had reached at Sedona that weekend? Where could we go from the top?

~~~

FOUR

The timid never find true love and happiness, but the bold do.
—Paul Twitchell, *The Flute of God*

THE GREAT RIFT

We went to the bottom. We went to the Grand Canyon.

With our friends Michael and Sharon and two others, Amy and Danny, whom we had just met, we drove to that great rift. We drove through a level piñon and juniper forest until the earth suddenly ended. Arriving at this world-edge, the lungs fill as one is hit with a strange mixture of fear and awe. Here you can see why Columbus's crew, and all who chose not to precede him, would fear the edge of the earth. Why would anyone in their right mind journey toward the void?

No one in their right mind would. But a true pioneer lives in a world beyond the mind, and sees the goal, not the difficult road to it. All of them, from Galileo to the Wright brothers, moved past the cries from the crowd: "Impossible!" "Blasphemy!" "Fool!"

At the Network Chiropractic Gate I had just attended, I heard a new song during a slide show. One line tugged at me: "Ships are safe inside the harbor, but is that what ships are for?"

Like Columbus (in 1492, some called him "mad"), we had just arrived at the so-called "edge." And, like many of the new worlds we would discover on our voyage, the Grand Canyon had its own set of rules. Crossing the bridgeless Canyon demands going into its depths, then climbing back out the other side. So, too, would the journey from our former life into the new.

But not yet. On that day, my obsession was the high view. I thought cosmic awareness was all I needed. No desire to tread the steep path into the canyon attracted me that day. But the little girl at my side—a brave voyager incarnate—had desires of her own.

"I want to hike into the Grand Canyon with Michael Stern and Sharon," Katie cried. I did not even reply. As I clung to my love of the high, expansive viewpoint, my tiny daughter asked to journey into Earth's heart.

Annie looked at me briefly, then turned to our friends. "Is that OK with you and Michael?" she asked Sharon. I couldn't believe Annie would consider it.

"Sure," they answered.

Ice covered much of the top of the Kaibab trail. I visualized our tiny daughter descending those steep, narrow switchbacks dropping into the Earth's great opening.

"Do you think she'll be OK?" I asked Annie. I clutched Andrew's hand near the five-thousand-foot precipice. An old and deep fear clutched me. I stood on that edge feeling fright that must have come from experiences older than my current mind and body could understand. Frightful, life-ending experiences that could have occurred at this very spot. While this apprehension did not overcome a desire to honor my daughter's adventurous spirit, I hoped Annie would be the heavy and say no.

"I don't know," she said, "but I'd rather have her die living, than live the living death of fear."

The woman I had married ten years earlier might have come to feel this way herself, but I would never have imagined her saying that about her four year-old baby girl. Annie had often seemed fearful and controlling, yet she was now calmly giving her child permission to hike into the Grand Canyon in winter.

So our daughter Kate, six weeks shy of her fifth birthday, skipped and hopped in hand-me-down sneakers over that icy cliff edge and into the Grand Canyon. Her father, still clutching his son's hand, replayed lifetimes-old memories of falling into that abyss. Tears filled my eyes.

I remembered dropping off my oldest brother, Bob, at Plattsburgh College. Suitcases were carted to the dorms. Then it was time to go. Mom hugged her first born, and hid her tears as we said goodbye. I didn't get it. But now I did. As I saw my little girl walk away without us, a weird combination of fear and sadness filled my gut. I understood my mother just a little better that day. Watching someone we love set off on their own journey hurts.

~~~

As I recalled those tearful initiations, I paced with Annie and Andrew along the rim of the canyon. The view was awesome—it was the lofty cosmic perspective that I so loved—but my daughter was a thousand feet below me on a trail not much wider than her three-foot height.

"It's freezing out here," Annie said. We stepped into the motor home. We made jigsaw puzzles with Andy. Big Bird's Birthday Party. Ernie takes a Bath. Annie and I took turns looking out the window, checking the trailhead, checking the clock. After Andrew tired of his puzzles, we tried playing cards.

Annie scanned the Grand Canyon newspaper. "Four people have died on the Kaibab trail in the past ten years," she said. We looked at each other, then checked the clock again.

"I can't stand this," I said. "I'm going down there." I laced up my hiking boots, put my jacket on, and started down the trail.

The path was dry and sunny after the initial snow-covered descent from the rim. Yet in spite of all of my early hiking and climbing adventures, this place terrorized me. Any slip on the trail would lead to a dramatic death in the canyon. My daughter was somewhere down there in tennis shoes.

About a half mile down, I heard an unmistakable sound on the switchback below me: Katie's high-pitched, never-ending chatter. The next switchback revealed a picture a tense father could never forget: Michael, Sharon, Amy, and Danny huffing to keep up with a feisty four-year-old. Kate was wearing a borrowed cowboy hat and a smile as broad as the hat's brim. "Hi, Daddy!" she said. Her beaming grin showed she hadn't any fear. To her, this big adventure was just another game, like Andrew's jigsaw puzzles. How wonderful to journey without question or fear.

We all hugged, then piled into the motor home for the trip back to Sedona. Our friends left for the Phoenix airport and their respective homes. We, on the other hand, returned to the same streamside site in Schnebly Hill Campground, perhaps more compassionate toward those in fear of others journeying toward the unknown, thanks to Katie's bold spirit.

FIVE

Lo the poor Indian! whose untutor'd mind
Sees God in clouds, or hears him in the wind.
— Alexander Pope, 1733

THE SHIP IN THE CLOUD

We hooked up the umbilical cords of power and water to our RV in the same site beside Cathy and Chris.

Each evening, around a crackling campfire, we got into long conversations about extraterrestrials, telepathic contacts, and signals of light. It seemed like the stars were watching over us as we talked. Cathy even showed us videotapes and carefully-typed transcripts of messages from her "friends."

My diary entries, which had for so many years reflected the dull light of despair over an often-troubled marriage with Annie and a constricting career, had brightened:

February 14, 1991
Sedona, Arizona

Overwhelming joy . . .
For the lack of fear, and for trust in life
For the blue sky
For joy

For my life
For this trip, watching Kate and Andrew bound around this campsite.
For crossing Oak Creek with Katie and then hiking straight up the embankment
For meeting a UFO contactee and her gentle husband
For Annie
Truth surrounds me.

~~~

Reading it over again, I was tempted to say that such a journal entry merely reflected the relaxed nature of someone on vacation in Sedona in seventy-degree weather in mid-winter. Undoubtedly, the educated, intelligent me would return to his senses. Yet a few days later, even as we drove across the bleak Midwest and back toward New York, my heart still sang . . . and something strange was going on.

That day, the motor home cruised silently at seventy-five miles an hour. With their numerous windows and doors and the aerodynamics of a soapbox, they are usually not quiet at highway speeds. They also guzzle gas. This day, our Travel-Master was absolutely soundless, and the gas gauge moved slowly as the miles piled up. Were the cosmic forces that had begun to touch us spiritually now affecting our physical reality?

As I stepped out of the RV at a rest stop, I was hit hard by a fifty-mile-an-hour west wind. It had been silently pushing us all day long, and had increased the gas mileage on our ten-thousand-pound beast by twenty percent. The logical me would dismiss the cosmic forces stuff, yet it seemed as if even our physical vehicle was reaping the benefits of our open hearts. The wind of Spirit blew with us. Something else stayed with us that day, too.

As we drove east on Interstate 40, I saw a cloud all by itself in the sky. The inside was bluish, and the outside was bright white. But I didn't think it was a cloud. It hovered at about eleven o'clock high as we drove through New Mexico. It hung in the same position as we passed through Amarillo, Texas and crossed into Oklahoma. I kept looking, wondering. There was something inside that cloud, but I didn't say a word.

"Do you see what I see?" Annie asked, looking up at the saucer shape inside the cloud.

"Yeah," I said. "It's been with us all day."

Annie and I looked at each other, smiled, then shrugged. I was so glad she had seen it too, because I thought I might have been imagining things. We drove seven hundred miles that day. That single cloud with the saucer inside stayed with us the whole time.

Two nights earlier, I had tried something Cathy shared with me in Sedona. I had called to the night sky, "Hi, I'm here. If you are really about truth and love, I'm here to help."

A bright light had suddenly appeared above me. Now this.

In my diary that night, after I sketched the saucer, I wrote, "This may be a new chapter in my life."

What new chapter? "Close Encounters"? "Mike's Imagination Runs Wild?" Two weeks earlier, I hardly even believed in ETs. Now I was seeing lights flashing in the sky and space ships hiding in the clouds. Was *this* part of a pioneer's journey? Did our world now extend beyond the confines of planet Earth, or was I just a flaking-out New York lawyer letting his heart lead him astray?

Flaky or not, I could make a decision. So could Annie. That night, as my family slept to the rumbling of diesel engines in a Loves truck stop in Oklahoma, I wrote:

After spending just two more days in New Mexico on our way back from Arizona, Annie and I decided we would move there. There is an inexplicable feeling there that we haven't felt anyplace else, even in Arizona. It feels like home.

SIX

There is no one who can return from there,
To describe their nature, to describe their
dissolution,
That he may still our desires,
Until we reach the place where they have gone
—From the tomb of Egyptian King Inyotef, circa 2,600 B.C.

BACK TO REALITY

My heart continued to soar with visions and feelings from the wide-open spaces of the West. This elation remained after we had arrived back in what I referred to in my diary as "dreary, cold, and ugly" Long Island, . . . but only for a few days.

After our return from that first scouting expedition, I shared my blissful feelings and our thoughts about moving to New Mexico with friends and family. Some rolled their eyes. Some said, "It won't work," or "You'll hate it out there." Others told us we would run out of money and be back in six months. Almost no one said, "Great!" or "Go for it." Some even said I was out of balance, "on the mental plane" or in "la-la land."

Their comments affected the new, soft-hearted me more than they could have before the trip. But their resistance failed to deter me. After all those negative responses, there was still one person with whom I looked forward to sharing these wonderful insights: my mother.

Mom had always been there for me. She even let my friend Michael Elrod and me bicycle two hundred miles to New Hampshire when we were only fifteen.

Years later, Mom cried when each of us went off to college, but she always put us first, knowing our adventures were an essential part of growing up.

So now that her son was a responsible father of two and a successful attorney, I knew she would be the first to support Annie and me in our decision to leave New York. I knew she would be the one to understand my compelling desire.

"It's easy to be happy and carefree when you're traveling around the country in a motor home," my mother said. "But when you get back to the real world, with laundry and dishes and work," she continued, "it's different."

~~~

Her words were like a blast of icy-cold headwind. I walked away from that brief conversation angry at my mother's anger. I did not realize at the time that sorrow sometimes hides behind anger's less vulnerable mask.

I should have understood, having seen my daughter off on what seemed to me like a walk into certain death. But my mother's reaction felt like a brick wall.

As if we had returned to a land of darkness, the old issues of a confused and scared husband soon returned to the pages of my journal . . .

March 17, 1991
Southold, New York

I was "down" today.
Doubtful. Sad. Angry.
In spite of all Annie and I have been through, I still have doubts about us. I'm not sure I love her. I don't think she loves me.

The spiritual heights I had reached out West lasted only as long as it had taken to plan, make, and return from a big cross-county trip. After our return, Annie and I talked often about moving, giving us moments of joy within the ever-present context of "reality." On most days, however, I bemoaned the fact that I still spent time in my law office (rarely more than a few hours a day, but even a few minutes was too much.) Doubts about our ability to really live without a thousand dollars a week tormented me. Maybe the practical critics and my good-hearted mother were right. Maybe we were kidding ourselves.

But something deep inside told me they were wrong. I knew about a life beyond the passive, unconscious drudgery that surrounded me. I replayed in my mind the feelings from that awesome trip to Arizona and New Mexico. I remembered the fascinating people we had met. No, I was not kidding myself.

I pushed into the headwind, and the "cosmic" stuff and feelings came around again.

March 22, 1991
Southold,
Things accelerating. Circles shrinking. A phone call from a friend. Talk of alien landings. Gem power. Light and Sound experiences. Network.
It feels like something BIG is happening to the entire planet. A major leap in consciousness or a major "visit."

I had no idea why these new aspects of life, especially the ET stuff, were coming into my world all of a sudden. Could travel alone have made my world grow so big so quickly? Dreams of spaceships and contacts, some so real that I included sketches of their shape, intermingled with the perpetual journal entries about Annie and me being distant so often.

Many nights, I dreamed of flying. Other dreams revealed our Long Island house twenty feet under the ocean, as if the sea had risen gently and left the house and neighborhood intact. Then more dreams of earth changes: I felt the earth shake and saw a fault line that split the continent right down the middle. Repeatedly, I saw the house in the high desert of New Mexico where we would live. Even from *there* I could see volcanoes in the distance filling the sky with fire.

Despite the graphic visions of my dream world, the feeling was never apocalyptic. I had learned in my spiritual studies that dreams were not always literal but worked as Soul's symbolic way of getting messages to the conscious self. Perhaps the "aliens" in my dreams represented alien concepts. Maybe the shaking and splitting of the earth stood for the polarization of my consciousness. Volcanoes for anger and rage released. Who knows?

There were other dreams and visions. During a contemplation, I visited a spiritual master at a teaching temple on the inner worlds, a magnificent, tall structure that rivaled any on earth. The inside of the building was lined with books like a great library. During that visit, I met the teacher in a quiet corner behind bookshelves and desks. He handed me a stack of books.

"What are these?" I asked.

"These are the books you are going to write," he answered. And the scene closed without another word.

Visions of traveling appeared, too, whether I was sitting to contemplate, driving my car, or scanning contracts in my office. I even saw mailing labels with our New York address on them cut in half, a dream symbol that New York was no longer my home.

Yet as these patterns of high awareness met the daily world, a painful, almost schizophrenic rift grew within me. The so-called real world felt less and less real and more and more painful in comparison to the "Altar of Light" I had visited in February.

Annie and I read books like *Essence,* by A.H. Almaas, and *Black Butterfly: An Invitation to Radical Aliveness*, by Richard Moss. Books like these set my head spinning even more rapidly that before. Annie, because of her early religious training, remained much more grounded than I during this strange time. She remained stable and on course, like a kite tethered by a string, while I, on the other hand, soared and dove and flapped in the wind like a kite released.

Each night, even if romance eluded us, Annie and I could still sit in bed and share our dreams and visions. "I can't wait to live in New Mexico where the sun always shines," she said. I could see that sun in her eyes as she spoke the words.

"I can't wait to live in the mountains," I said. "Every time I'm up there, I feel so energized."

Then each morning, my heart sank. "Do you think I'll be able to sell my house?" a client would ask. "Do you think you could get them to kick in another hundred bucks on that termite clause?"

That world was now unreal and irrelevant. Normal events and concerns felt painfully trivial compared to the awesome love and interconnectedness of the Universe. I felt like Alice in Wonderland, where absurd places and events around me were what everyone else considered normal.

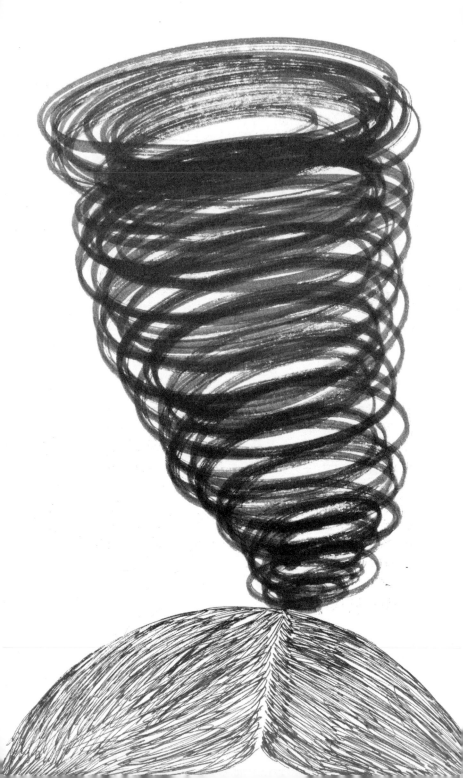

SEVEN

Think back over your lives for the last year or two and realize that there have been times when you have been in incredible chaos of consciousness. You have been in a chaos of decisions about who you are, where you want to live...
Barbara Marciniak, *Bringers of the Dawn*(199<u>3</u>)

THE VORTEX . . . AND THE MESSAGE

By March of 1991, Annie and I had completed two trips to the Southwest. Dreams and bedtime conversations about moving there added some lightness to our usually lukewarm marriage. But they were not enough to overcome our deep problems or my self-analysis about our every move. I had become tormented by the contrast between my day-to-day reality and what I had come to know, and between my visions of what our marriage could be and what it was. On top of that, I had begun to examine the whole idea of moving. I lived with a swirling vortex in my head.

THE VORTEX

March 22, 1991
Southold

[On this date, though we had already put fifteen thousand miles and stickers for about twenty states on our motor home, I wrote, "PIONEER JOURNAL BEGINS"]

Spinning head, confused heart.
Am I a suburban boy playing pioneer, or am I an alien to suburbia chasing visions of heaven?
Am I looking for love with Annie that's not meant to be?
Is this a cycle or a sign?
There is a frontier. There is light ahead. Light all around. It is a frontier of choice, or choices. One can choose to just go on or to open up and move up.
In the human state, one heart cannot be shared by all, so people suffer. In the God state, all is one heart, so all radiate love.
Am I on the true road to God state?
Is my heart pure?
Have I abandoned Annie? Have I given up on love in my own home?
I let Kevin Costner into my heart tonight for three hours while watching Dances With Wolves. Will I let Annie in for three minutes?

Around and around I spun in the days after that second trip West, whirling between this new cosmic consciousness and pretending to care about the mundane. Cosmic visions vs. a sink full of dishes. Changes in the Earth vs. changes in someone's will. Floods and droughts vs. profits and bankruptcies. Around and around. Annie and I shared our new thoughts with each other, but everyone else doubted or scorned us. Well, not everyone.

During this confusing and frightening time, Annie and I still made weekly visits to Donald Epstein's chiropractic office in Bellmore. On one visit, though I had not said a single word to him, Dr. Epstein showed me that I was neither alone nor invisible in my confusion.

He touched my neck gently. Then, with a broad smile, asked, "How's life in the vortex?"

In the Network model, the chiropractor feels the tone of both the spine and meninges. By "tone," I had learned, they meant not just its tension, but also the actual tune or "song" it played. I had no idea Epstein could hear the churning torment of my thoughts, my cacophonous symphony. How could he possibly know? But he did. Tears filled my eyes.

"It's a bitch," I said, forcing a smile.

Not another word was spoken. Dr. Epstein continued with his adjustment. A sensitive friend had touched me, and by touching, understood.

As I left his office that day, Donald Epstein asked, "Do you know why angels can fly?"

"Why?" I asked him.

"Because they take themselves lightly," he giggled.

~~~

THE MESSAGE

The vortex, he said. Our life was spinning like Auntie Em's house in the twister. And it was because Annie and I were following a message that had been streaming through for several years: *"Follow your heart."* The message. It came in the books we read, the lectures we attended, and even from movies we watched with our kids.

"Let you heart guide you," said the mother dinosaur to her baby in *The Land Before Time*. It was the same message I had heard in *Field of Dreams* ("Have you ever been this close to your dream," Ray Kinsella asked Doctor Graham holding his thumb and index finger a quarter inch apart, "and let it slip out of your fingers? Some would consider that a tragedy.")

Field of Dreams played softly on the big screen, yet I walked out of that theater feeling as if someone had grabbed my heart with two hands and yelled, "Michael, wake up! Follow your dreams NOW, before it's too late!"

I heard the message in *Dead Poet's Society*. "Carpe diem!" the teacher played by Robin Williams told his students. "Seize the day!" Then, as if I needed to hear the message yet another way, I heard it loud and clear at a writer's conference in Boston.

One of the speakers there, a beautiful, almost translucent woman whose young age belied her wisdom, said, "When you fail to follow your heart, you will feel a deep sense of loss." She went on, "When we let opportunities pass by, the feeling in our bodies is similar to the feeling when someone close has died."

I had felt that feeling, that empty, sick feeling in my stomach, too many times to have to analyze her words. The message struck me, then stalked me, for much of 1989 and 1990. Every book, every movie, said "follow your heart" and spoke directly to me as Soul.

Even *The Little Mermaid*, a sweet, romantic fairy tale, shouted to me. When Ariel sang, "I don't know when, I don't know how/ but I know something starting right now/ watch and you'll see, someday I'll be part of that world," I cried like a baby. I went back to the theater alone to watch it again. That little mermaid was singing *my* song. *I* wanted to be part of another world.

Those films and words magnified the impetus to change our life. I had to get out of my law practice. Annie and I were both inexplicably drawn towards the Southwest. And, other than the words of those who had a stake in us staying, the messages universally and unequivocally said "DO IT!"

And the mother dinosaur in *The Land Before Time*, carried the message a little further.

She did not merely say, "Let your heart guide you." she added, "It whispers, so listen closely."

'Twas my next step, then, to listen to the whispers of my heart.

~~~

EIGHT

If you are not willing to change and not willing to give things up, you will have to go through experiences that are less than joyful.
Barbara Marciniak, *Bringers of the Dawn*

THE PERFECT PLAN

And the whispers said, "Go, go now while you are young and healthy. See the country. See where you will live . . . GO!"

So my wife and I planned a third scouting expedition across the heartland of America and into the Wild West.

Annie and I didn't whisper. We talked about it day and night, obsessively, some said. We studied road maps and books like *Best Places in America*. We sought word from fellow travelers, as those who moved West a hundred years before us must have.

"What's it like out there?" we asked. "What are the people like? How is the weather? What's winter like? Is it hard to get over the mountains?"

We also asked questions our forefathers were no more likely to ask than questions about life on other planets: "How are the schools? What are houses going for? What are your annual taxes?"

Then, with maps, magazine articles, and the *World Almanac* laid out on the kitchen table, we plotted out a detailed itinerary.

"First," Annie said, "there's the Network Transformational Gate in New Jersey on July 8th. We can make that our first stop, then head out on the Pennsylvania Turnpike. Then we can take I-70 through St. Louis to I-44, which'll take us to I-40 into New Mexico." After two years of traveling solo as a college admissions counselor, she had become as adept with a map as Wyatt Earp was with a gun. Annie could navigate a trip to anywhere.

"Then after we leave New Mexico," I said, adding a personal preference to our plans. "We can head up through the Rockies and check out Colorado Springs. According to this book, it has low housing costs and a strong economy."

"How many days of sunshine does it have, Michael?" Annie asked seriously. "I want a sunny place."

After several evenings like this, our expedition itinerary read like a blueprint: Six weeks. Ten thousand miles. Long Island to New Jersey through Pennsylvania to Albuquerque to Colorado to Yellowstone in Wyoming and Glacier National Park in Montana. Then up into the Canadian Rockies, east across the Trans-Canada Highway, and back into upstate New York. Two days here, three days there. Eighteen hours to get from here to there. Each day planned.

On July 10th, we would leave the Transformational Gate in Princeton. On July 13th, we would park at the American RV Park at Exit 160 of Interstate 40 just outside of Albuquerque. Perfect plan. Perfect order.

~~~

NINE

July 11 Passed 15 graves . . . made 13 miles
July 12 Passed 5 graves . . . made 15 miles
July 18 Passed 4 graves . . . made 16 miles . . . "
—From the diary of Cecelia McMillen Adams, who took a
wagon train from Illinois to Oregon in 1852

DEATHS ALONG THE TRAIL

July 11, 1991 8 A.M.
Minneapolis

*In our TravelMaster motor home on a residential street in
Minneapolis, Minnesota. Andrew's sleeping. Katie's watching
Muppet Babies. Annie's getting dressed.*

Minnesota?
We started as planned, at the Network Chiropractic Transformational Gate in Princeton, New Jersey. But something happened there that changed everything. As I wrote in my diary,
the event, and particularly the room in which seventy-five
people were being adjusted simultaneously, felt "sacred."
  The people, the feeling in the room, and especially the love
and focus with which each doctor worked, overwhelmed me
with a sense of divinity I had felt only a few times before. New,

too, was the chain of inner events that followed this profound moment. The diary entry looked simple enough. But the feeling nearly killed me.

First, I was moved to tears at the holiness around me. Then without warning, an emptiness—an abyss no smaller than the Grand Canyon's—sucked me into a deep chaos. If I could experience such profound spiritual connectedness sitting in a square, concrete, carpeted hotel conference room, I reasoned, then outer religion—even a great one like the one I practiced—was meaningless.

Suddenly my beliefs about overtly sacred places and people were banished, and a huge, gaping gulch confronted me. In that moment, in that moment of awakening to a sense of the sacredness of *any* place, I fell over the edge of that dreaded canyon and died. Could Mark Twain have known that one's *religious beliefs* could die from travel?

And if such profound holiness could be found in a place with such a brief gathering of unaffiliated people, and if religion itself were scrapped, what could possibly be so special about a cathedral, a mosque, or even the Temple of ECK? The temple had recently been built in Minneapolis by Eckankar, the teaching I had held dear for the previous fifteen years.

A few of the people attending the Gate could relate to my dilemma. Of such a holy place, one said, "It's just like any other building." Later that day, I confided in an old friend about my new viewpoint and the resulting void. "Why don't you come up to Minnesota and feel for yourself?" Michael Stern suggested.

After a confusing afternoon spent in the devastating ruins of my belief system, I sought out my wife. "Annie, I'd like to go to Minneapolis tomorrow," I said. I was really thinking: *What about our neatly planned trip?* Our timed-to-the-second itinerary? Annie's detailed, multi-colored, highlighted road map?

"OK" she said casually. For me, transformation had brought with it destruction and chaos like the winds of a hurricane. For my wife, the winds of transformation had made her flexible. At eight A.M. on July 11, 1992, the second day of our spontaneous visit to Minneapolis, on a warm and humid morning, I wrote:

The Temple of ECK seemed almost void. After what I've experienced these past few months, the outer Eckankar teachings, and the temple itself, seem empty.

How could it have been any other way? I had entered the building with the new conviction that no place was any more special than another, and that no religion was sacred. Yet I felt sacrilegious as my pen touched the paper. The emptiness I felt in that building may have been *my* emptiness, but the philosophical reason failed to soften the feeling. There, in the upper bunk of my motor home, I cried. Inside, I felt empty, dead. My eyes burned. My stomach ached. I mourned the death of some of my most cherished "knowing." Later that day, in an attempt to regain my footing, I returned to my closest, most unconditional friend, my journal:

So start again, Michael. Learn what is REAL. Learn to be HERE. Learn ESSENCE. Radiate spirit in the moment . . . from within, not from an outside source.
Someone at a recent seminar said, "If your anchor point is anything other than Spirit itself, you are in for a rough ride."

Spirit, itself. No outer source, no sacred texts or buildings . Essence, the only real thing. Spirit itself.

"Soul searching" has a whole new meaning for me today. Behind distractions, behind my hyper busy-ness and future/past focus is something scary, something I've felt in fleeting moments of peace.

Why scary? Because living in it requires giving up all present and former beliefs, self-image, world-image. Because change can hurt.

We left Minnesota that day. The gas tank was full. My tank of knowledge, and my heart, felt empty. Like the early pioneers, at that point in our journey we had no choice but to bury our dead, and kept moving.

~~~

. . . All along the road up the Platte River was a grave yard; most any time of day you could see people burying their dead, some places five or six graves in a row, with board head signs with their names carved on them.
From the diary of Jane Kellogg, 1852

July 12, 1991
Culbertson, Montana

Waking dream—a long, tiring day driving across North Dakota. Long, tiring.

In two days we covered twelve hundred miles. The traverse across North Dakota and Montana seemed endless. Smooth asphalt wound through endless prairie, marked only by a house every several miles, and by white crosses placed where an incomprehensible number of people had died on this straight, level, unpopulated and intersection-less road. After we had passed maybe the fiftieth cross, Annie and I gave each other a puzzled look . "Car accidents?" she asked me.

"Here?" I said. "There's nothing or no body around to have an accident *with*."

In some places, four or five of the white crosses, one or two smaller than the others, stood together. A family?

In the 1850s, a cholera epidemic swept the world. It hit the westward-moving pioneers hard. It was estimated that there was a grave every eighty yards for the twenty-four hundred mile length of the Oregon Trail. Annie and I saw nearly this many grave markers as we crossed northern Montana. The crosses were all fresh and white. It was impossible that they were from the early settlers. Some even had plastic or fresh flowers on them. Were Annie and I, 139 years to the day after Cecelia Adams had logged the number of deaths and graves she saw each day, witnessing the results of a plague?

"Only drunk driving could have caused so many deaths on such a straight and empty road," my addictions counselor wife declared.

"But there are so many," I said. "It seems like there are more crosses for the dead than people living here."

We stopped for gas and groceries in a little town.

"What are all those crosses for on Route 2?" I asked a friendly check-out clerk. The answer confirmed Annie's theory. This trip had opened my eyes to how only the *mode* of death had changed during humanity's century-and-a-half-long journey into "modern" times. Other things had changed, too.

If the nineteenth century pioneers had the luxury of taking a pre-move scouting excursion, the same trip from Minneapolis to Glacier would have taken three months. Three months over a rutted dirt trail. No graded asphalt. No screen windows keeping out the hordes of thirsty mosquitoes. No air conditioning (it reached 102 degrees as we crossed Montana).

They would also have been hauling burlap sacks containing their ever-dwindling supplies of the flour or corn meal, and walking beside the wagon trains stuffing the empty sacks with buffalo chips to fuel each night's fire.

Their journey might have also taken them into mid November, when early winter storms often brought death as effectively as a case of cholera or a sharp arrow from a Pawnee bow.

For the four of us, it was just two long, boring days crossing the prairies. Bathroom on board. Cabinets stocked with food. Grocery stores never more than a meal away. Cold snacks in the fridge. Hot meals in the oven. Yet many had died on this trail. Somehow, with the inner deaths haunting me since my experience at the Gate only nights before, I wondered if a quick scalping would have hurt any less than the death of my spiritual belief system. First, I would get to spend a week in Eden. Then I would find out.

TEN

A spiritual path is not a home; it is a road home.
—Marianne Williamson, *A Return to Love*

INTO A MAGICAL LAND

July 14, 1991
Glacier National Park, Montana

Another long day. I felt. Yesterday I felt in my stomach the way it feels after a good friend dies (me).

Today, in addition to that sadness, anger filled my day. The know-it-all Mike Hall died in Minnesota. I don't know if the grieving has just begun or is over. Today, I know nothing, and I feel angry about that. But not so angry that I want to go back.

When the pioneers confronted death among their wagon train companions (which they did on an almost daily basis), they broke ground when they could, laid a marker, and moved on towards what the early travel guides assured was a paradise. They pushed on towards their new life there. After our first night camping on the east side of Glacier National Park, we crossed the park, and the Continental Divide with it.

On July 15, 1991, we pulled into the Avalanche Creek Campground within Glacier National Park. We had driven through snow fields and waterfalls and rainbows to get there, through a place I called "beautiful beyond beautiful."

Shortly after we had parked the RV, I watched my children talk with deer in a forest of thousand-year-old cedar trees. Katie and I hiked and saw a mother deer with three brand new fawns.

The four of us hiked through the forest, crossing a log bridge over roaring, blue-green rapids. Deer roamed to our left and right, and I later wrote, "It feels that the mountains are watching and vibrating for us." It felt like we had stepped into the real Shangri La, into a very special corner of the earth.

As we hiked through that place, I learned that that particular section of Glacier Park, because of its high rainfall and its position between several tall mountains, had been spared the ravages of forest fires over the past thousand years. The place was literally protected from the world around it . . . and I could "feel" its wisdom as I walked its ground.

Yet even as I listened to the trees tell their ancient tales and breathed sweet, magical air, the "trouble" in this paradise loomed over me. The deep "connectedness" with the life around me I felt in Avalanche Creek stood in stark contrast with the lack of connection I felt with the one I had long referred to as my "inner guide."

I strolled through a heavenly forest, but thought how I had been kidding myself for the second half of my life like so many "devout" religionists who claim to "know the Lord" but are really just full of words. This thought felt like yet another blow to whatever ego may have remained in me.

From there, I moved rapidly to feeling as if my feet were touching the ground and that I was on the right path for the first time in my life. What did that say for eighteen years of studying one religion as the "only" path to God? I felt angry at myself for being so narrow-minded for so long.

Then I remembered: my studies had taught me that there is always a plus element, and that the purpose of any true teaching is to take the student to the point of individual mastership—beyond the path itself. Perhaps those many years were more fruitful than I realized.

~~~

That evening, just before the sun turned Avalanche Creek from day heaven to night paradise, we took Andrew and Kate to what the National Park Service calls a "fireside talk." Ostensibly, the ranger's talk was about the flora and fauna of the park, but a short side note struck me.

As we gathered on log benches around a fire, the park ranger told us of the original meaning of the Great Divide or Continental Divide. To the ancients and the early explorers, the divide meant more than the mere place where water flowed either to the Pacific or Atlantic oceans. "The old belief," the ranger said, "was that, as one crossed the Continental Divide, the old life was left behind and a new one could begin."

I knew what he said was true.

~~~

As we prepared to leave Glacier National Park, I felt grateful for having been given two days in one of Earth's special nooks. Places like this have a power that surpasses their scenic beauty; they are of Spirit itself. They are what religion and holy structures try to be. They have the wisdom of a million winters and summers, and days of sunshine and wind. Their river's sing a song even more timeless.

Everyone should visit there: the spiritual power of places like Avalanche Creek brought out in me an intense desire to share their magic with those who may be rushing to an appointment or "killing" time in front of a TV.

Some people find a Shangri La-like this (or a religion that feels right) and stay there. But in staying, their world view narrows, until they confuse their small piece of Earth with the true grandeur of the universe. By clinging to the snapshot, they miss the feature. A spiritual path is not a home; it is a road home.

We travelers had soaked up a magical few days in Glacier the way leaves soak in sun. New life. New food. New energy. Unlike our green-leafed brethren, however (and in keeping with our true purpose) we moved on . . . into *more* worlds of wonder.

~~~

July 18, 1992
Jasper National Park, British Columbia

As we drove north into Canada, Glacier National Park stood serene, blissful, even hallowed in my heart, like a small, secret chapel within a great cathedral, or a secluded, moss-filled grotto just outside the great marble walls. Walking into such a place is prayerful in itself, and listening to the voice of God in that place is a holy act.

The Canadian Rockies, in contrast, shout their sacred song. "I'm glorious!" they cry. "I'm beautiful!" Many travelers go as far north as Banff, a magnificent place where elk run wild near town and glacier-capped mountains fill the horizon. The road north of Banff, however, heads into the rougher, wilder Jasper Park.

During our two-hundred-mile drive from Banff to the town of Jasper, elk grazed in every field we passed. Through icy mist past green-cold lakes we moved. "Look, Michael!" Annie shouted. I pulled over quickly.

"What is it?" Andy asked.

"It's a bear!" Katie said. A black bear rummaged for termites in a log just thirty feet from us. We stood just outside the motor home door.

"It's coming this way!" Annie said, herding us up the motor home steps.

Later, as Katie played in a small park near a campground, a large elk jumped toward her. An hour or so after that, we stopped to greet a family of mountain goats at roadside. Suddenly, one of the sweet-looking but horned creatures lunged toward Katie. My heart stopped as I watched the animal lower its head and charge full speed at my daughter. Annie and I watched helplessly, too far to be able to grab Kate or divert the mountain goat.

The goat stopped its attack six inches from Kate's rear end, and Annie and I laughed as a near catastrophe brushed by.

"Look out Dad!" Katie yelled. "There's a mountain goat attacking you!"

I turned around. A furry white head, pointing down in attack position, was charging me at high speed. I had nowhere to run, so I just stood there, frozen, watching the goat. At the last second, this one changed course, too, barely brushing past me.

A few miles farther up the road, Katie pointed, "There's another bear!" We stopped to watch that one walk through a wildflower field and into the woods. It was not even noon yet, and I felt like Swiss Family Robinson in the jungle. We approached a stopped car near a bridge. A roaring waterfall had formed a deep gorge. Nine bighorn sheep stood on the cliff edge just below us. After several minutes of admiring their rugged beauty, we watched them walk to the top of the waterfall on loose-shale cliffside trails that no human could negotiate.

As we had not had enough adventure that day, as the mist burned off , the exploring family parked at the foot of the Athabasca Glacier. A short hike brought us up to a giant snow field, where a snowball fight seemed surreal and I became a human sled on which Kate and Andrew slid down the glacier.

Every minute that day filled me with awe; my sacred places had grown immense. We parked the motor home that evening at a secluded place on the banks of a fast river. As the sun slipped behind fourteen-thousand-foot peaks, the river reflected the sky's glow. Andrew and Kate played with us on the river's edge until the last light was gone. I felt some frustration as I realized that the two-dimensional videos we took would never capture the feel of the glacial mist, the cool of the rivers, or the mountains' magic.

At midnight, as my wife and children slept in our covered wagon in the black wilderness, I clicked on a dim light and grabbed my journal:

July 18, 1991
Jasper Park, Canada

By thoughts, crazy. By feeling, great. I can feel the mountains; they literally move me. When I feel them, my abdomen waves, my cells rejoice in near ecstasy.

Yet I know this is just the beginning. I know there are holes—places in me where feelings have not reached for most of my life.

I remember one scene in <u>Return of the Jedi</u>, where Luke Skywalker looks anxiously into a dark, deep hole. He asks Yoda, his master, "What's in there?"

"Nothing you don't bring with you," Yoda replies.

I have many such caves. First I shall discover each one, then explore their depths right to their source. Then, I shall feel the feelings in each cave, grieving losses, feeling stabs and thrusts of thought-swords.

Then, one by one, fill each hole, each crack, with light. Love, that elixir—light, love, Spirit, Eck, Holy Ghost, Universe, God, Sugmad, whatever—shall then reside in me. I shall be it. No leaks. No holes. No caverns hidden by empty thoughts, words, deeds.

The gray of dawn glows behind the mountains to the east. My ears ring. My body vibrates.

~~~

ELEVEN

In Endymion, I leaped headlong into the sea, and thereby have become better acquainted with the soundings, the quicksands, and the rocks, than if I had stayed upon the green shore.
—John Keats

THE PIONEERS MEET MORE RUGGED FOLK

So noble, so "spiritual" were the thoughts and words that filled my diary those days. Two days later, as we pioneers wandered southward out of the incredible Canadian Rockies, we pulled in to the only campground we could find that provided the water and sewer hook-ups occasionally needed to keep the TravelMaster and its crew traveling.

"Yuck," I groaned as I observed what looked more like a grass parking lot crowded with trailers than the isolated, forested spots we had camped at for many nights.

"It's only for one night," Annie consoled me.

As I struggled to squeeze the RV into a cramped alleyway between two trailers, a man emerged from one of those rigs to assist me. After ten minutes of tiny back-and-forth moves, I had finally parked and shut off the motor home.

"New York," said the man, observing our license plate. "You're far from home."

"About three thousand miles," I answered, though I didn't feel far from home at all.

"Come over for a beer after you get settled."

"Sounds great," I replied. I hadn't had a beer yet that year. But I reasoned that a graceful acceptance to this man's hospitality might make the evening at this place which felt like Manhattan after our nights in the wilds of the high Rocky Mountains.

Kate and Andrew had wasted no time heading for the swings. Annie stood with two people on the far side of the campground. I showered, then hesitantly knocked on the man's screen door.

Twain said that broad viewpoints come from travel itself. But our compulsory stop in that little municipal campground taught me more. That evening, as I shared a beer and sausage pizza in a trailer filled with strangers, I learned that awakening could occur in places neither mystical nor spiritual on their surface.

July 20, 1991
Incredible. Cranbrook, B.C.

I just had a beer with John, Elaine, Mal, and Trish and their daughter, Sheri. John and Elaine live near the Arctic Circle in the Northwest Territories. A different world.

To get home from their "southern" trip to British Columbia, they must travel a thousand miles north from Edmonton. The last four hundred miles are over gravel road, then they often risk their lives crossing the "ice bridge" over the Mackenzie River, hoping to make it.

They live in the dark all winter. The temperature hovers at fifty below zero. It's light all summer, so they sleep little then.

As I sat in a small trailer with John and friends, Annie talked with a Yugoslavian couple who live in the Yukon. He works on radio towers forty feet in the air in eighty-mile-an-hour winds and seventy below zero temperatures.

I was a more humble traveler after my close encounter of the third kind with those "aliens." From my little life in New York, I had never conceived of people living like this in the twentieth century. I thought only the early pioneers lived such harsh, high-risk lives.

The folks back on Long Island had repeatedly told me I was crazy for leaving a successful business and for stepping away from "essentials" like income, comfort, and medical coverage. What would they make of those rugged Canadians, who take their lives in their hands each time they leave their house?

~~~

With this humbling new wisdom taken on board in Cranbrook, British Columbia, we once again moved onward. At our last stop in Canada, we picnicked on a hill overlooking a lake. From where I stood, everything around looked and felt heaven-like. Yet Heaven is no place to stop. So that Eden faded into our rear-view mirror as we continued our journey.

At the tiny town of Porthill, Idaho, we smiled at the customs officers and drove on. We stopped for gas, and Annie meandered over to a farm stand, where she picked up a quart of fresh huckleberries. Their sweet, black juice left an all-day trace on Kate and Andrew, who, I noticed, were beginning to yawn or go "ho-hum" each time Annie or I said, "Look at that!"

At the ripe old age of four, Katie in particular had become jaundiced, numb to the beauty. By contrast, I was now feeling the same sense of awe in a grass lot in Cranbrook, British Columbia as I did in the shadow of a thousand-year-old tree or when the black bear had headed directly towards us in Jasper National Park.

We circled Coeur d'Alene Lake, then wound our way back to Interstate 90 for the drive through southwest Montana toward Yellowstone. I took notes:

July 21, 1992
Pipestone, Montana
Sunrise

Heading to Yellowstone today. Funny, it doesn't really matter where I am anymore. Yellowstone is no more exciting than this flat, grassy campground in Pipestone. Both are wonderful places to be, to meet real people and to get back to essence.

It is wonderful to be here. It was wonderful to make eye contact with those elk, deer, and bighorn sheep. Wonderful to feel mountains and trees, to meet people who live in another planet — the Arctic Circle — and love it.

There's more. The last time I spoke with Michael Stern (it has only been three weeks but feels like three lifetimes), he reminded me not to accept a "pretty good" answer to the multiple choice questions about Life, but to get to the answer.

I shall.

So, since it mattered little where we were, I tucked my pen into my diary that morning, unplugged the motor home, and moved on. Ostensibly, we were heading towards Yellowstone, the first, and considered by some the greatest National Park, yet this scouting mission would continue to show me wonders within myself that no atlas or guidebook could foretell.

~~~

July 22, 1991
Yellowstone National Park

Before the kids woke up, a light fog filled the meadows. Annie and I drove into the park and saw a herd of elk, a herd of white-tail deer, and a lone mule deer. Then our two pajamaed little ones walked out from their rear bunks and pointed to two bull elk up the hill. Just then, a herd of bison crossed the road in front of us.

That same day, in the midst of that living, misty magnificence, I wrote of feelings as diverse as the landscape of Yellowstone National Park. For we, like these coarse planes of Life, encompass so much more than pleasant panoramas or wonderful wildlife. Gurgling streams, blue lakes, and green trees entwine with steaming geysers, boiling mud holes, and a harsh, even grotesque landscape. A camping trip with spouse and two children, too, came with its hot side. That night, after Annie had blasted me, I wrote:

Exhausted. Annie steaming mad. Me inconsiderate or giving up. I invited some campers into our motor home while she slept in the upper bunk. When the people left, Annie blew up. She may be showing me that I tend to allow outsiders into the intimate part of our life too readily (when I act out of the old social consciousness).

Michael Stern makes me squirm and I like it. Annie makes me squirm and I do not. It feels like downbeating instead of a challenge.

Twain was right: travel increases opening/change/challenge experiences a hundredfold. This, combined with the Essence work I am reading about in A.H. Almaas' book by the same name and Mike Stern's "tests" (multiple choice or not) puts Marine boot camp in baby league.

Right now I feel tired, as if more than my body has been climbing in high elevations all day (we're at eight thousand feet here at Canyon Campground). Working. Moving. Moving. Moving.

My last entry that late night had no connection with the park, the animals, or the bitter argument Annie and I had before she went to sleep. The sentence stood all by itself at the end of the page:

Santa Fe is in first place, whatever that means.

~~~

TWELVE

There was a white man who boasted that he would kill the first Indian he saw, he soon had opportunity of fulfilling his boast as they saw a squaw and he shot her as he would a wild animal and the Indians came on and demanded the fellow to be given up and they had to do it and the Indians skinned him alive.
—The diary of Helen H. Clark, 1860

BRUSHING SHOULDERS: A SCALPING FROM A WHITE MAN

It was that white man's arrogance that brought on his gruesome death. The rest of his wagon train traveled through the same Indian country in peace. Now it was my turn to be called out from my wagon train.

We stopped at a playground in Jackson, Wyoming. I sat down near a man seated at a picnic table. The small talk had lasted maybe two minutes.

"Are those your children?"

"Yes. Yours?"

"Traveling." "Pastor." "Lawyer." "Writing a book." Despite the cordial conversation, I soon noticed that fear had gripped my chest —the same fear I felt each time I appeared before certain judges. As the conversation continued, I felt tense, nervous, and physically cold.

As soon as I had said two words about *Flight Lessons*, the small talk was over. My use of the term, "New Age" turned a chat in a pastoral setting into a scalping.

"New Age?" the pastor said, eyebrows scowling. "I think the so-called 'New Age' is nothing more than a commercial rip-off. What do you believe in?" he asked me, and, "What is grace?"

"I believe I am an eternal part of God," I answered. He glared.

"You cannot mean 'eternal.' Only God is eternal," he scorned. "You must mean immortal."

"No. Eternal," I said. And I believe those may have been the last words uttered by this ambushed traveler.

"You believe you are *eternal*?" he questioned, leaning toward me. "Then what were you two thousand years ago? Or I suppose you believe in past lives." I did, but it didn't feel like the time to say so.

Though he kept on talking about Christ, I knew Jesus never acted that way toward anyone. So I sat there, mute. I felt the way I had felt once when, as a fourth grader, my father confronted me after I had been caught breaking bottles on the sidewalk. When my father had looked me in the eye and yelled, "What do you think you were doing?" I had just shrugged my shoulders and sunk deep into the cushion of my chair. It was one of my first experiences in leaving my body. But I could not respond to his question.

Twenty-five years later, my wife of ten years rested in our motor home and my own children played on the swings. I had not committed any senseless act of vandalism or done anything wrong. Yet as the pastor's inquisition continued, I sat there just as mute. Then, after expounding about original sin and needing Christ as the only savior, he scolded me for my speechlessness.

"You call yourself a lawyer and yet you have no logical answers?" he said with a haughty smile. "How did you ever graduate from law school?"

The Indians who had skinned that white man not far from where I sat had had just cause, but the man across the picnic table from me seemed to relish his put-down, the way the skinned white man had undoubtedly enjoyed his slaughter. His joy came not from his desire to teach about Christ or to be loving, but from what he obviously saw as his mental or religious superiority. Behind my fear, silence, and inability to respond, I felt great contempt for this pontificator.

Days later, I realized there was much to be grateful for in my chance meeting with that man of God. His pressing for answers to his religious questions made me realize that I *had* no answers. He had also served as a dramatic example of how study and knowledge of written theological works—how ideas and beliefs alone— can make one arrogant . . . and empty.

I wondered if my "beliefs," as he called them (he kept saying "we Christians believe this" and "we believe that") were as barren and weak as his. He thought his foundation was right. Meeting him made me realize I had no foundation at all, that whatever "beliefs" I might have held had literally vanished in three weeks of traveling.

Two years after that rough encounter, I attended a spiritual seminar. The speaker talked about those who had reached Cosmic Consciousness (Whitman, Thoreau, etc.) but who had failed to keep moving on to God Consciousness because they lived alone. The speaker continued, "When people 'bump the ceiling' and don't keep ego in control, they look down on others instead of seeing them as lights of God."

In my early spiritual practices and after my first two Network Transformational Gates, I had "bumped the ceiling," experiencing the grandeur of Cosmic Consciousness. Whereupon, I immediately looked at everyone who lacked my great awareness as some sort of cave-dwelling Neanderthal.

The speaker at that seminar, mirroring the travel quote from Twain, closed his talk by saying that because of modern travel, we can "brush shoulders" with many people, thus avoiding the trap of high consciousness which had caught many great beings. Travel. Brushing shoulders (shoulder pads, anyone?) Moving on to God Consciousness. Moving on.

The Reverend Bill Jones, by merely being himself, convinced me that my spiritual journeys must continue beyond the land of arrogance. (It is interesting that our meeting took place at an elementary school. Perhaps that is where we both belonged, spiritually speaking.)

That pompous man inspired me that same evening to write part of the preface to this book. As offensive as he was, he truly did act as an agent of God that day. For upon seeing how loathsome a spiritual know-it-all could be, I conceived a new prayer: "May I never be as tight-minded and 'right' as Reverend Bill Jones. May I learn to radiate God's love."

~~~

Two days later, we pulled out of Jackson and motored out of southern Wyoming. We twisted and wound over an exhausting series of steep switchbacks on a surprisingly spectacular Route 191 in northeastern Utah. Then the winds of change came.

In the town of Vernal that summer evening, Kate and Andrew played miniature golf for the first time. As we played under the blue Western sky, a wind blew up from the west. It quickly grew into a howling gale. A minute later, I turned. Andrew was whisked off his feet onto the plastic carpet of the miniature golf course, a light victim of a heavy wind. The "wind" of the

Reverend Bill Jones had knocked me over just a few days before. The winds of change touch and move children, too.

We moved on.

~~~

THIRTEEN

"My Guide and I crossed over and began to mount that little known and lightless road to ascend into the shining world again . . . until we reached a point where a round opening brought in sight the blest and beauteous shining of the heavenly cars.

'And we walked once more beneath the stars."
—Dante's *Divine Comedy*, just before leaving Hell

AN INNER MEETING WITH MY FATHER

We left Utah and drove east through high desert. We toured Dinosaur National Park, then headed further into Colorado. As the afternoon waned and I tired of driving, we sought our night's camp. Sometimes when we're tired, we quit too easily. We almost stayed at an ugly campground in Craig, Colorado— a crowded, commercial one.

"Let's go a little further," Annie said. "I'll drive." Annie drove an extra hour. As she drove, we climbed in elevation. In a space that might have taken the pioneers four or five days to traverse, we had left the barren, high-desert lands behind. We stopped to witness a brilliant double rainbow arching for ten miles. Then, because Annie wouldn't settle and drove that "extra mile," we found a national forest campground situated at nine thousand three hundred feet with hundred-foot evergreens all around. And, once again, we had crossed the Great Divide.

Katie and I hiked together just before sunset that evening. Through pine forest and alpine meadows we walked. We felt raindrops fall from a clear sky. We followed deer tracks along an abandoned road, but saw no deer. I turned around as we walked and saw perhaps the most vivid picture of that entire awesome journey we had started weeks before: Our motor home, sitting in the distance, dwarfed by towering pines and the lofty Rocky Mountains, a tiny traveling ship in an immense, gracious universe.

As if that sight were not enough, suddenly my often-blasé daughter said, "It smells nice here by these wildflowers, Daddy." At that moment, I inwardly thanked Annie, and God, for bringing us to that place.

~~~

The beauty of that evening poured into me, calming slightly an inexplicable anger that had been shadowing me like a tiger stalking a stray deer. I did not understand the feeling, so I could not address it. As the forest glowed outside my window, I grabbed my journal. After jotting notes about the drive, the double rainbow, the feeling of anger, and Katie's comment, I wrote:

July 27, 1991 2 A.M.
Steamboat Springs, Colorado

In the eyes of an infant, or of a puppy, or in the gracious shade of a tree, is something that cuts, sometimes painfully, through the outer layers of our being. We can avoid this depth for our whole lives, but once felt, our shields from its intense love are no longer friends, and must fall.

The "Law of Silence" may be less about keeping things to ourselves and more about listening. "Listen closely to your heart," the baby dinosaur's mother said. "It whispers."

In this high forest, a tree stands so close to my window I can hear it. A lone star winks at me through its boughs.

Oh, Universe, oh Universe, continue speaking, singing, to me that I might learn to listen. To listen unfettered by filters of mind and personality. I shall reveal the tuning fork that is me to the resonance of you. I shall open the valves of this flute of God to the Golden Wind, to the breath of the gods.

I feel at one with past, present, and future right now. Why did the Anasazi disappear in A.D. 1200? What happened to the dinosaur? At one with past, present, and future. No distinction, no extinction. I hear the dinosaur's heartbeat. I dance and cook with the Anasazi. I fly with the eagle, catching prey with loving talons.

I needed psychologist John Klindienst to point out what I was doing when I moved to Southold ten years ago and how I let that step toward independence be undone. The move to Utah in 1974 (when I chose to go far away to college) was undone by insecurity (as I raced back to the comfort of my girlfriend).

The steps being taken now are — rather seem—more important: the entire Universe will be affected by what happens next. This next book, this "pioneer's journal," shall reveal my searching, groping, tripping for that which envelops and fills me.

I have "enough," but I cannot leave it alone. I have an abundance of love, peace, money, and sunshine. Yet the search continues.

I finally fell asleep after sharing those diverse, ethereal feelings with my diary. Four hours later, I heard, "It's time to get up, Daddy."

"I'm hungry," Katie said.

Annie and I served cereal, cleaned up, and moved on. That night, we camped even higher, at ninety-six hundred feet, ten miles east of Aspen.

July 28, 1991
Twin Lakes, Colorado

Just a few days ago, I wrote about the two meanings of the Continental Divide. Last night we slept right on it, on the line that connects the East and the West, the old life and the new. And it felt that way. On our way to this camp, we crossed the Divide several times again. Are we moving through life so rapidly?

Again that night, as my wife and children slept blissfully in the cool, high mountain air of Colorado, I sat at the kitchen table haunted by the feeling of anger that had followed me deep into the forest. I stared out the window at the hulking shadows of tall pines, and heard not their celestial voice this time, as I had the night before, but a critical, human voice. The voice which spoke did not take on the guise of a blue-auraed inner master or spiritual guide, but of my father. I felt so angry at him, the embodiment of my own inner critic, for stepping on my "high consciousness" in that beautiful setting.

"All this spiritual stuff is great, Michael John," I heard him say, "but you have to live in the real world." I thought as he said it that it was a lot of shit; I fought with these thoughts, and spoke back to the voice inside.

"But when I think of great people, Dad," I countered, "like Thoreau, Bell, Lincoln, Edison, or Disney, they are the ones who followed their hearts no matter what, not just when they could pay the bills." As I argued with that fatherly image inside, I knew that my choice of great people reflected my bias toward free thinkers and doers. Not good enough for the critic.

"But you have two children," he poked.

"So? Should children only have parents who suppress their dreams? " I asked. "The outer person, the me living the easy, comfortable, lawyer lifestyle, is so very unreal to me now."

"Is that what you're running away from?" he asked.

"I'm running away from that mock-up," I cried. "This is not a psychological cover-up for my insecurities. It's deeper than that. I wonder who I am. I wonder if I can face myself, or God, naked of my thoughts, my cute personality, and my words?"

"So ask your questions and *keep* your job!"

"I can't. I have kept myself so busy thinking and worrying about things like money or appearances that my deeper, un-mentionable worries hide behind the smoke screen."

I was stronger on the inside than I had been with Bill Jones or could ever be with my real father. Before that 2 A.M. debate with my "Dad" voice, my "right brain," faded into the woods that night, I said "Go to Hell!" to that inner critic. I knew the time had come to work past the pitter-patter inner chatter of "reality" of "You have to live in the real world, Mike." And I knew that the anger was giving me the strength and momentum to do it. *It was time to pioneer into what was truly important.*

Two days before that middle-of-the-night inner conflict, at a wonderful place in Jackson called the Bar-T Ranch, I heard Bill Thomas tell us how his grandfather had set up a homestead in Jackson in the mid-1800s.

"He came over that pass right there," he said, pointing to a nine thousand-foot rise to the west. "My grandmother said it took twenty-one days to go fourteen miles. 'On some nights, we could throw a rock to the previous night's camp, we made so little progress,' she told me."

Mr. Thomas continued with his real pioneer story. "They lumbered all winter using bow saws and horse-drawn sleds," he told us, "then milled the timber in the summer with a steam-driven saw."

"They raised goats, chicken, some cattle, and vegetables, and used these to get through the long winters," he went on. "They lived real well." He closed with a proud smile, his eyes gleaming.

During his talk, Bill Thomas also said that his grandfather had "caught hell" from his family for leaving the family business in Salt Lake City back in 1853. As I beheld the mountains his grandfather finally settled in, as I smelled the tall pines and heard the rushing river below us, I felt that Bill Thomas's grandfather had caught Heaven instead. He had struggled over mountain passes, and left behind a known, predictable life in Salt Lake City for the truly unknown.

I could only marvel as our "covered-wagon" motor home crossed that very same pass in Jackson, Wyoming in fifteen minutes. Yet even as I marveled, taking none of our modern comforts for granted, I knew there were other passes to cross. And I knew that I must leave the safety and comfort and predictability of my present life in Southold, Long Island to seek and set up a new life in an unknown place.

~~~

After that argument with my inner critic and my recalling Bill Thomas's story, though it was the middle of the night, I clicked on a dim light and quietly opened to the first available page in my rapidly filling journal.

So I must log the journey from the relative known and comforts of my present life as a lawyer in rural Long Island to something else, to the unknowable. Annie and I now live in what is practically a physical paradise: The weather is friendly and moderate, the grass and trees radiate a lush green and offer comfort and shade. The nearby bays change color with the movement of the sun each day, the moon each night, and the seasons each year. But something is missing.

This journal, it would seem, cannot begin with the escape from the torment the Pilgrims left, or the famine of late nineteenth century Europe which drove millions of immigrants away from their homes.

I lack those overt afflictions, yet I am tormented by the lack of life around me, and I hunger for a food not growing in the thick soil I stand on. I feel driven to this New World, whether I ultimately find it in Southold, in Santa Fe, or in my own heart's "back yard," as it were.

There's no place like home. There's always more. Move on. Move on.

~~~

FOURTEEN

*Now shall I sing that second kingdom given the soul of man
wherein to purge its guilt and so grow worthy to ascend to
Heaven.*
　—Dante's *Divine Comedy, Purgatory*

PARADISE, TO PURGATORY, TO HELL, AND BACK

Purgatory. "An intermediate state after death for expiatory
purification." Expiate. "To put an end to. To make amends for."

　—*Webster's Ninth Collegiate Dictionary*

Travel. Rapid transformations and perpetual paradox. Hotels
to holy places. Temples to turmoil. Dreams to deaths. Ministers
to monsters. Heaven to hell. Paradise to purgatory.

July 28, 1991, the same day that had started with an angry,
solo battle at 2 A.M., turned out to be one of the most fun days
of my life.

After a relaxing morning in the campsite, we drove the hairy
thirty-five miles over twelve thousand-foot Independence Pass
(and the Continental Divide!) to Aspen. Though the single-

lane, two-way road made my hands sweat and my legs wobbly, the high drive showed me a sky so blue it seemed unreal. And that deadly road led us to a Sunday in Aspen.

Andrew and Katie and I floated balloons in a fountain of water. A Texas clown widened Katie's eyes with magic and mime and balloon twisting. Then, while Annie and I sat in our choice of warm sun or cool shade and shopped in flashy stores, Katie played on the playground with a boy from Hong Kong and Andrew made a friend from Switzerland. Hang gliders flew over Aspen mountains as we drank "solar shakes."

There at the foot of Aspen Mountain we ate a four-star lunch at Lauretta's sidewalk cafe, where Andrew flirted with a sweet hostess. Later, as Katie and Andrew waded in a fountain pool, Annie shopped, and I watched all the beautiful people stroll by.

I played all day, forgetting about justifying my life choices, grateful for the joy and beauty around me. From that heavenly paradise called Aspen in July, we drove south. We landed, of all places, in a town called Purgatory.

~~~

I had pictured Southern Colorado as high desert. Instead, our last night there was spent at ten thousand feet among lush grass, tall pines, and shimmering aspen.

After a great breakfast, we rode horses through the mountain forest at Purgatory. Katie rode a horse called Boots, Andy rode Pocahontas, Annie rode a pinto named Freckles. My lessons would even follow me into the mountain wilderness of the Colorado Rockies: There in Purgatory, I rode a sweet horse . . . named Preacher. I laughed when the wrangler told me my horse's name. I knew it was no accident.

The ride, thank God, was smooth. This horse was so much gentler than the preacher I had met the week before in Wyoming.

~~~

From our cool ten-thousand-foot camp in Purgatory, we headed toward what would be our third Network Transformational Gate. For notwithstanding the obliteration of our original itinerary, we could still arrive in central Arizona on the day of the Gate.

We cut through a bleak corner of New Mexico and descended down to the fire and brimstone called Phoenix in July. The thermometer read 114 degrees. Even with the air conditioning on high and the shades down, we couldn't get the inside of the motor home below ninety. Just being there was a challenge for us all.

I questioned myself on my reasons for attending another Gate, and the brutal heat brought the test beyond the philosophical firmly into the physical.

I went to that first Gate in Sedona in February for two reasons: 1) During Network adjustments by Michael Stern only seven months ago, I had reached "cosmic" highs, but Michael had said there was more, and 2) we happened to wind up in Sedona the same day as a Gate — which was, to me, an obvious gift.

At that Gate, I experienced the high states I thought were the self-realization and God-realization states I had read about for many years. Yet I had learned in the months since that Sedona Gate that enlightened ones are those who have tasted the "sweet nectar," the "Divine Spirit." And, instead of drowning in the intoxication of it, they work hard to live up to their desire—no, their inner mandate — to live and share it on a day-to-day basis.

So I chose to attend another Transformational weekend because I had become aware of patterns within me that were preventing Spirit's flow. I wondered how such a weekend would appear to the readers of my journals in a year, or in fifty years, but I went anyway.

As the seminar started, my wondering ceased. After my first adjustment, I felt that I encompassed the entire universe. Feeling that connection, I cried in agony for how I had dishonored my Universe. I cried for scarred, mutilated Earth, for slaughtered animals, for neglected souls. I felt their pain. Their pain was my pain. All distinction vanished.

Although this was the third Network Chiropractic weekend I had attended, and though my uncle and two older brothers were chiropractors, I had trouble understanding how a simple touch could bring such experiences, such perspectives. In his talks, I had heard Dr. Epstein, the founder and developer of Network Chiropractic, say that the purpose of the chiropractic adjustment was merely to "free the spine and nervous system of interference," but it felt to me like I was an antenna , able for the first time to receive signals that had passed by for most of my life.

~~~

After sobbing for gratitude during my first adjustment, there was more. More signals were being received, more emotions felt, and more inner suffering lingered.

Saturday afternoon, after I had completed three such intense Network "clear outs" as they are called, I met a man named Rick Moss, who teaches "Pre-cognitive Re-education." Before we had spoken a word, he saw through me. He saw my confusion and terror and tightness. He *saw* them. Before his workshop had even begun, as I stood in front of him, he said,

"You have work to do, my friend." As he said this, he pointed to the chronic, nagging tight spot in the center of my chest. I had given him neither verbal nor any other indication about it.

He, like my friend Mike Stern, said I had more "stuff." I wanted to deny it, but I knew that even after having reached high states of being, this stuff had to be faced, felt, experienced, accepted, lived, and released. I did not even know what "it" was.

On Sunday morning, the clear-outs felt more intense than ever. I thought I had reached "God-realization" during my first gate in February. How could there be *more*? During one adjustment, though it took place in a cool, air-conditioned hotel conference room, I soaked my shirt with sweat, and drenched the adjusting table with tears.

As it was happening, I thought it was profound release. It was not: profound *resistance* created that heat, just as electricity travels coolly through a cord but produces heat in the toaster's resistant element. I had simply cooked in the heat of my own resistance.

Sunday afternoon, I attended Moss's second session. I entered the session at the tail end of the previous group. The hole/knife-point area at the base of my sternum burned in pain. I overheard Moss helping others as they were asked to let go of certain dark spots forever.

"Let go of your abandonment," he said to them. He was addressing a group of at least a hundred people, yet I felt him speaking those words to *me*. How did he know? During the session, Moss walked over to me said he sensed *my* pain as abandonment. After that, I felt I could began the process of letting go.

At the close of the weekend, Dr. Epstein addressed the group. "Remember, he said, "that this weekend is called a Transformational *Gate*, not a transformational finish line."

The audience laughed, but as I felt the paradoxical combination of ecstasy and terror in my body, I knew I was once again entering uncharted territory. There was more to face, to feel, to accept, and to release. More unknown, inner wilderness to seek, discover and master. I closed my diary entry after that profound weekend thus:

So, in spite of the extreme comforts of 1991 (at least, compared with the early pioneers of the wild American West), I know I am a pioneer of my own wilderness. I accept the fact that wild, dark creatures roam where I am about to tread, creatures whose strength and cunning has been nurtured by my denial of their very existence.

I am a modern pioneer, advancing toward my own essence.

FIFTEEN

Now while the great thoughts of space and eternity fill me I will measure myself by them,
And now touch'd with the lives of other globes arrived as far along as those of the earth,
Or waiting to arrive...
—Walt Whitman, *Leaves of Grass*, "Night on the Prairies"

HARMONICS OF FREQUENCY MODULATION, or EXTRATERRESTRIALS REVISITED

As we traveled more, the parallels and coincidences got pretty weird. When we had left Arizona in February of 1991 and headed for New Mexico, we had met Cathy, the alien contactee. Two days later, Annie and I saw the saucer-shaped ship in the cloud.

When we left Arizona after that Gate in August of 1991, we again headed for New Mexico. We arrived in Albuquerque on about August fifth. We drove around for two days and said, "Yeah, this is a good place to live." Then we drove north on I-25 from mile-high Albuquerque, up La Bajada ("the descent") to Santa Fe, at seven thousand feet, and into our friend Robin Ann Hunter's driveway.

We attended a public HU Song held at Robin Ann's home. We sang the HU (pronounced like "Hugh") for about twenty minutes. The HU is called a love song to God.

After the HU, Kate, Andrew and I returned to our motor home, which was parked in Robin Ann's driveway. As we peered out the window of the motor home, waiting for "Mommy" to come tuck the kids in, we saw a man approach Annie as she walked down Robin Ann's driveway. A button down shirt and pressed slacks covered his six-foot-tall frame. He appeared to be in his early fifties. His hair was cut short.

"Here," we heard him say as he handed Annie a stack of papers a half-inch thick. "I think you might find this interesting."

"Thank you," was all Annie could come up with as she accepted the papers from the stranger and continued walking toward her waiting family.

She did not know him. Nor did I. No talk other than social chatter had preceded his gift. He did not give copies of the document to anyone else. Just Annie.

"What did that guy give you?" I asked as I anxiously took the papers from Annie before she had even stepped foot in the motor home.

"I have no idea," she replied. "You tell me."

"It says, 'The Pleiadians, through Barbara Marciniak.'" I said to Annie as I read the cover sheet. "The title is 'Harmonics of Frequency Modulation and the Human DNA.'"

"What the heck is *that*?" Annie asked.

"I don't know. It's dated November 15, 1990," I said. "It's only eight months old. Whatever it is, it's probably fresher than some of the packaged foods in our cabinets."

I read aloud to Annie as Kate and Andrew listened: "The Pleiadians are a collective of extraterrestrials from the star system of the Pleiades . . ."

"You mean people from outer space, Daddy?" Kate asked.

"That's what it means," Annie answered. "Let Daddy keep reading." So I did.

"'The Pleiadians are now here as ambassadors from another universe to help Earth through her difficult transition from the third dimension to the fourth dimension and to assist each of us in our personal endeavors of awakening, remembering, and knowing.' What did he give this to you for?" I asked Annie. "Were you talking about ETs or UFOs or something?"

"No," she said. "I have no idea. And it's not like he was giving them out to everyone. He only had this one copy."

"Maybe it's just part of our 'charmed life,'" I joked.

I flicked through the papers. The transcript included questions from the audience at Stanford University, where the channeled lecture had taken place. Someone asked the ETs, "I have a question about commitment, and about what you mean about impeccability." The answer from the alleged star beings surprised me.

"In a short period of time, there is going to be a great need—a great realization —of who is a keeper of frequency, and who is just shouting B.S. Because the keepers of frequency are going to be called upon to create a certain stability upon this planet. And the keepers of the frequency know 100 percent of the time that they create their reality, and they do it 100 percent of the time . . .

"That is the depth of impeccability and the depth of commitment that we are speaking of . . . . We are here to remind you of who you are and what you have agreed to do— what you have come here to achieve on this planet."

Their short answer on commitment and the word, *impeccability,* did not sound like the kind of stuff I would have expected from an "ET." I more expected talk about spaceships and funny-looking beings than about commitment to creating one's own reality.

"What else does it say, Daddy?" Katie asked.

"It says, 'We are here . . . to encourage you to remember . . . so that you can discover for yourself the miracle that awaits.'"

"That awaits where," Annie asked impatiently. "From the spaceships? From the sky, what?"

"From Mars?" Andy laughed.

"Inside the human body," I read

"Wow. That sounds like what Donald Epstein was talking about last weekend," Annie said. "He said something like, 'The answers are in your body.'"

"And remember when Epstein talked about the 'tone' or 'frequency' of the body," I said. "And how the frequency of a person in a deep meditative state often matches the resonant frequency of the planet Earth. Check this out. It says, 'We said that information is stored in bones, just as information is stored in stones — by sound—by frequency.'"

"And listen to this," I exclaimed. "It says, "'That is why we have been recommending for quite a long time now to get body work.'"

Having just come from an intensive weekend of body work, and having experienced what felt like a literal re-tuning of my body, the strange pieces and coincidences were beginning to connect.

Six months earlier, in the same area, it had been a cloud. That mysterious cloud with a blue-gray saucer shape inside had made Annie and me give each other puzzled looks, but it was probably just a cloud. On this day, mysterious as it was, it was something we could hold in our hands; it was a forty-five page typed transcript.

"What do we have to do with the Pleiadians?" Annie asked.

"And why did this happen in Arizona and New Mexico?" I asked. I wondered why we had been drawn to those places by dreams and visions in the first place, and why these strange events had occurred after two intensive weekends of body work. The questions seemed weird and endless. But at that point, we were pioneer explorers on a scouting mission. We moved on.

~~~

SIXTEEN

"If you want to get clear—if you want to understand yourself and your universe—go spend a week or two free from electricity--in a place of nature , where you are nurtured, and you are having a good time.
—Barbara Marciniak, "Harmonics of Frequency Modulation and the Human DNA"

CLEAR

On August 15, 1991 we arrived "home" in Southold, New York. We had just returned from *six* weeks free from electricity. And we had lived almost entirely in places of nature, where we felt nurtured, and where we had a good time. I looked dreamily back at Glacier National Park, Jasper, and playful days in Aspen. We had also attended two chiropractic weekends whose purpose was to "clear" the nervous system. Were we "clear"?

For most of that fantastic adventure, the answer was an unqualified yes. But being clear brought on a new perspective as we returned from that second long trip, a perspective that was not easy to stomach: New York had never felt so bad.

It no longer felt like home. And, just as it had after we returned from our first trip West, in the face of family and friends, my head swirled with questions and judgments. I re-examined what was really important. I wondered what the 'true' spiritual path was. And I questioned whether people were crazy for digging in their heels where they were (both in place and in consciousness), or whether I was crazy for blowing with the wind.

I felt sane, not crazy at all. Yet I felt like withdrawing from the people around me, the local Kiwanis Club, and from every other group in the world. In some ways, I felt like leaving the Western world's "normal" life, and the mass consciousness, like the hippies of the 1960s and 70s had.

At the same time, unlike the hippies, I did not feel like dropping out of society as a form of acting out. It was just that buying into that belief system had kept many doors closed, and stepping away from it had opened me more to the universe, to the Light and Sound of God. Little by little, even before we moved West, while we still lived in rural New York, Annie and I were breaking away.

First, we made changes in the house. For months before our journeys, Annie had been saying how the television irritated her. But I watched it habitually, especially during those late nights when we slept apart. The trip gave the kids and me a break from that pattern, like an alcoholic without alcohol. We had brought our little twelve volt TV/VCR on our trip, but never took it out from under the motor home's couch.

Within a few days after our return to Southold, the television in the den was on again. Sometimes I would sit there with the remote and just click and click and click until my eyes (or my thumb) gave out. It felt offensive, but I sat there anyway. Annie had barely tolerated the boob tube before our trip. That day, she walked into the den with the Pleiades article in her hand.

"Listen to this, Michael," she said with a smirk, reading from the transcript. "The intent behind your television was to create a nation of automatons—to create a nation of humans addicted to the frequency that was broadcast to them, so that even if they didn't like what they were seeing, they would still stay there." It sounded so right on, I did not even want to argue with her. So I didn't. She continued anyway.

"And get this," she added, running her finger to another paragraph in the transcript, "Television is one of the paradoxes where liberating information is broadcast through a disruptive frequency."

"So there you are," said Annie, still quoting the article, "you are watching television and some show is telling you how uplifted and how unlimited you can be—while subliminally you are being hit with a frequency that keeps you from original thinking . . . that keeps you in a survive, arrive, be on time, be silent, go to work society."

"And there's even more," Annie said, gleefully quoting passage after passage of reasons to get rid of the omnipresent television. Then she dropped it.

As if Annie's bodily and intuitive feelings were not enough, as if the unequivocal statements by the Pleiadians hadn't driven the point home, later that day I bumped into an electrician friend who was wiring musician Billy Joel's new house in nearby Southampton.

"You should see some of his sound equipment," he said. "But you know what's interesting, he doesn't own a television. Billy Joel said it stifles creativity."

Within a day, we banished the televisions.

"Here, Mom," I said, as the first was summarily delivered to my perplexed mother. Another, likewise exiled from our home, rode in the trunk on its way to Annie's parents. We kept the portable TV/VCR that could run in the motor home, but in that vehicle it stayed while we resided in the house.

The day after we had excommunicated our televisions, I wrote:

The house immediately changed. I told Annie it felt like the roof was removed and the house was open to the stars. Annie said a "fog" had been lifted.

And we both felt an incredible, new power yesterday, as if a new level of cosmic force had been accepted. This, in turn, opened things up even more. Annie actually talked to me this evening about flying—actual, unaided physical flight—as if it were as normal as taking a walk.

Changes began happening all around. A few days later, the coup occurred in Russia and Hurricane Bob came through. It was time for me to change, too.

A few days after that, I visited with my sister, Nancy. I rambled on about our "great adventures" and "spiritual awakening," she stopped me.

"Listen," she said.

"What do you mean?" I asked, forgetting in that moment that Mike Stern had told me the same thing just he day before.

"Just listen," she said looking me straight in the eye.

Later that same day, I drove over to my brother Rick's office. After getting off his adjusting table and waiting for him to finish with his last patient of the afternoon, Rick and I talked for a half hour. Instead of blabbering about my trip, I heeded my sister's advice; I listened. I let myself be vulnerable. He criticized.

"I understand you have a new religion now," he said in an angry tone. I listened. As he talked, he reminded me of some things I had said in the months before I had met the Reverend Bill Jones, that I had spoken some critical, smug, and judgmental words. They were coming back that day as I remembered to listen. It was learning time.

In the face of my family, I felt less than cosmic. On August 24, slightly more than two weeks after "enveloping the universe" during a transformational weekend, I wrote:

No Guru, no Master, no path have I. No teacher, no father, no mother, no teddy bear have I.

Life isn't about saving my family, or the world. There is an even bigger world out there.

How may I pioneer into this world?

SEVENTEEN

I'm writing a letter to Daddy.
—Bette Davis in *Whatever Happened to Baby Jane*

SHARING MY NEW REALITY

Of all the difficulty, the self-doubt, and the endless mind chatter I had created and endured from the time Annie and I had begun to follow the strange call to the Southwest, nothing obsessed me more than the desire to make my family of origin understand me. Whenever I sat in the same room with a parent or one of my brothers, particularly after the initial reactions to some of the "cosmic" and "ET" statements I had made, I made the smallest small talk I could manage.

Weather, jokes, and fishing results. Never consciousness or earth changes, and never ever the kind of personal feelings of change and doubt that filled the pages of my journals. Though I did not know how to speak to them, I still wanted them to understand my reality.

I gritted my teeth and maintained a self-confident, know-it-all exterior each time I saw one of them. Yet I grew tired of hearing bits and pieces of second-hand criticisms and first-hand innu-endo about my lack of mental and emotional stability.

I just wanted them to understand me. I craved their approval, their support, and their love the way a puppy does. Without those things, even with the team strength Annie and I had built as we prepared ourselves to leave a familiar world, I felt like an abandoned puppy. And I felt like I could not leave with so much misunderstanding around.

I decided to go out on a limb. I would share *everything* with my father, mother, sister and brothers. And I would do it in one grand never-happened-before Hall family meeting, which I would call. I would sit with them and tell them about my cosmic experiences, my rational deliberations, and even my feelings about *them*.

"I'll clear the air, even if they do ridicule me," I said to Annie.

"If that's what you want to do . . ." she said.

"Just the fact of my sharing will touch them," I replied. "They might even gain some respect for me."

Many of the writings from the early pioneers came not just from their diaries, but from letters they wrote to family back home. So I ventured into my faithful diary, and wrote a letter to the family that seemed far away:

August 30, 1991

Dear Family,

During the past two years, and particularly during the past eight months, profound and strange experience has become a near-daily part of my life.

I have bathed in white and yellow light, felt charges of electricity flow through every cell of my body, and seen things I would have never believed myself.

Some of these experiences happened during Network adjustments, but many — most—have not. Some have occurred while Annie and I held each other, while traveling, and at other times more and more frequently.

Some of you have been thinking, "What the hell is wrong with Mike John?" Your thoughts are like words. I can now hear them and feel them. Whatever they are, be assured that I can handle them and that I would prefer honest, "outer" communication.

In anticipation of some of your questions:

Yes, I do have a different religion now. No, it's not Network Chiropractic or Michael Stern-ism as some of you have said. In a way, I hope, it's the same religion of Jesus (who wasn't a Christian) and Paul Twitchell (who wasn't an Eckist). It is direct and powerful.

Also, I'd like those of you who need to think that I'm crazy or kidding myself, that I am healthier and more conscious than ever.

My first book will be published next year and the second and third right behind them. I've known that for quite a while now, but not everything can be shared.

Many of you keep making comments and innuendoes about the "real" world and getting "back" to it. I am learning that the real world is pretty vast, and that obsession with houses, cars, food, and money has become as absurd to me as I guess I have become to you.

Some of you have also made comments about the fact that Annie and I have paid Network Chiropractic over two thousand dollars to attend three Gates, but you are paying the manufacturers of your cars like Mercedes and Lexus ten or twenty times that amount, and that just keeps you hooked and distracted for a few more years. Or how about paying five thousand dollars a month to a bank on your mortgage, as Annie and I used to do. Are we crazy for giving that up?

And the letter went on:

"Yes, I know there's some righteousness in what I am saying, but I love you guys, and I need to say this stuff right now. And, no, you don't have to go to "Gates," but I can tell you that they are a wonderful opportunity that has touched all of our lives.

How do I close this "speech" to my family, who thinks I've lost it?

There's Kahlil Gibran's story of the wise king. The people all love and respect this king. A witch places a curse on the kingdom's well and, one by one, everyone in the kingdom goes crazy. The king has his own water supply and is unaffected. The people start talking about how "different" and "crazy" the king has become and plan his murder. Finally, the king drinks from the tainted well and the people rejoice that he has re-gained his "sanity."

I have decided, even if I seem crazy to you, that I'm not going to drink from the well anymore. I love you all."

"What a great letter," I thought. Wouldn't I show them how strong and sane and forthright I was. And how wise. In three days, a family gathering would provide the perfect occasion to sit my family down and tell them all my profound tales.

September 2, 1991

Rick's birthday. Party at Mom's. All gathered. I didn't read the letter.

That was the whole entry that day: "I didn't read the letter." I wasn't ready to face them. I had chickened out.

A few days later, after having been home from our eleven thousand-mile trip less than three weeks, Kate, Andrew, Annie, and I climbed aboard the TravelMaster once again. This trip would be just a "hop, skip and jump" of about two hundred miles to the Catskill Mountains in upstate New York. Yet I would attend our fourth Network Transformational Gate so that I might travel further . . . into the realms of what the Pleiadians called the "miracle that awaits inside the human body."

The sharing of my reality with my family would have to wait. More adventuring into the unknown beckoned.

~~~

EIGHTEEN

It is love of the adventure and the tremendous intimacy of sharing and receiving at the very boundaries of our being that enlivens me.

—Richard Moss, *The I That is We*

LIGHTNING, AND LOVE

September 8, 1991
Phoenicia, New York, Pathworks Center

We arrived Friday afternoon, driving through modest stone gates into a valley more idyllic than any I had seen in my perhaps fifty-backpack trips into the Catskills. Deer roamed freely and without fear, just as they had in that special corner of Glacier National Park. The air smelled of apples and freshly mowed grass.

People walked the beautiful grounds and hugged old friends. Annie spotted Donald Epstein and his wife, Jackie, walking up a stone path. We hugged, there in the lush, cool mountains of New York, having seen each other just weeks before in Phoenix.

~~~

Saturday morning, fifty chiropractic adjusting tables were set up under the blue sky on the Pathworks Center tennis courts. This time, no overtly profound experiences occurred during my time on the table, but the weekend included various other classes that took place between chiropractic adjustments.

I walked up the hill from the tennis courts to the meeting house for a "rebirthing" breathing class. I had thought that rebirthing was some kind of therapeutic or hypnotic regression into one's physical birth experience. Hardly. To me, the process felt more like hyperventilating on purpose.

The coaches started by having the class (there were about seventy of us in the room) lie on their backs on the floor. Then we were shown how to breathe fairly rapidly in and out through our mouths until, the coached said, "the breath takes over and the breathing becomes automatic." That was all there was to it. Just breathe.

So we started. After a few moments of breathing, the sensation felt like the uncomfortable light-headedness that occurs after you blow up half a dozen balloons. Then I felt "pins and needles," first up my arms, then throughout my entire body. After that came nausea. I quickly opened my eyes, looking over the heads of seventy people on the floor breathing heavily for the nearest garbage pail. Fortunately, I did not need it. That stage passed in just a few moments.

As to what happened next, my diary entry merely read, "New levels of transcendence. New levels of sensation." But it could have filled pages.

I turned face down to the floor. In that moment, I embraced the entire planet Earth. I could actually feel and encompass the entire planet and everything on it. Then the floor disappeared from under me, and I floated in a sea of stars. The earth had become just one of millions of dots of living light in the universe. Then things got *really* weird.

As I lay on the floor in that room filled with heavy breathers, powerful charges of electricity tore at my chest from the inside. Not only could I feel them, but I could *see* what looked like yellow lightning bolts exiting through my rib cage.

Although I was in no physical pain, I let out a blood-curdling scream from the sight. Anyone outside of the building must have thought some medieval torture was going on inside. I was just breathing hard, watching and feeling lightning shoot from inside of me, and screaming loudly in the terror of the experience.

As I continued screaming, the coach gently tapped my shoulder and suggested I turn over. As soon as I did, I stopped screaming and resumed the rhythmic breathing. Suddenly, I felt a connection with the sky, and had the feeling of missing my home there. I cried softly.

From that way-out state, I could hear the room quieting down. One of the coaches said aloud, "You can finish up and come back whenever you're ready." Slowly, I opened my eyes, looking at the ceiling as if checking to see that I was still on Planet Earth. Then I touched my body to confirm that I still had one. As I sat up and finished weeping, the first person to come into view was Ted Robinson, a trial lawyer from New York. He smiled gently at me from across the room.

I had met Ted at the Gate in New Jersey in July. Back then, we had compared lawyer stories. He knew how I was leaving my small-town, non litigation practice. I learned that he lived fighting in the trenches of the matrimonial trial parts of the tough New York court system. He was a lawyer's lawyer. I despised lawyers, and lawyering.

Just after our eyes met, he crawled through the crowded room and hugged me. After the drama of the previous hour, I melted in the comfort of his fatherly embrace. At that moment, I almost felt that I was in the arms of God. I then stepped into a paradox that had me bursting with raucous laughter as suddenly as I had started screaming just moments before: "God in the body of a lawyer." Given my feelings about lawyers, it was the funniest thought in the world. And it was *true*. Ted and I laughed hysterically for long, joyous minutes.

"Was that you I heard screaming up in the meeting room?" Annie asked later that afternoon.

I told her about the connection with the universe, the lightning in my chest, and about "God in the body of a lawyer."

"I could hear your screams all the way down the valley." she said. She said she understood. My parents and siblings waited two hundred miles to our South. Would they?

~~~

The power of the weekend followed me from the mountains as we drove our motor home back over the Hudson River and Long Island Sound bridges Sunday night. I knew my own challenge of addressing my family awaited me. And I felt myself cycling through that spiritual vortex called "Chaos" again.

Things in our old world seemed more and more absurd to me. Not bad, as they once had, but absurd. As with the king and the tainted well, I had resolved not to drink from the tainted well anymore, so I felt out of place. The kind of socializing Annie and I had mastered in the previous ten years suddenly felt like a waste of time and energy.

What did feel good were those random or spontaneous meetings with people I might or might not know, especially when I practiced the listening Michael and Nancy had told me to.

Those interactions, so much more than the old patterned ones, seemed to involve a more free transfer of energy.

I wrote some of those chaotic thoughts into my journal:

September 18, 1991

Living here seems absurd, too ("here" could be Southold or Santa Fe or Colorado Springs). This state I am in now — this "no-old-stuff-fits-anymore" —carries with it a new responsibility, for if I can no longer keep myself busy in the "normal," social consciousness, then my INTENT must be clear and pure, lest I rot in an empty, self-made hell of separation.

All that is left now is an intent by this speck of life to serve Life, period. This is no longer frightening, but this transition period has been tough. I feel physically and emotionally exhausted right now.

Even if I am making a total ass of myself in the eyes of my family, I do not think I should ever regret having taken this journey from the safe, "normal" life . . . to the unknown.

As I kept feeling out of sync with "normal," I breathed relief in words I had heard Donald Epstein speak during the Gate. "Normal," he said, "is a setting on a washing machine."

I felt more like I was *in* a washing machine; my dirt was constantly floating to the surface. The arguing with my father, which had started in the mountains of Colorado, had become a constant thing. As I lay in bed at night, I would hear him say, "What do you think you're doing with your life?"

Then I would blast him, attacking his life-style and his daily routine. I fought this inner battle on a regular basis, attributing comments to my father that he had never spoken, then blasting him for having said them. When I actually saw him each day in the office, I could only make small talk, because I didn't even know where to begin.

NINETEEN

"The bond that links your true family is not one of blood, but of respect and joy in each other's life. Rarely do members of one family grow up under the same roof."
—Richard Bach, *Illusions*

A MONKEY IN THE TREE

September 20, 1991
Southold, New York

I can talk about anything and everything with my wife. I can talk to trees, animals, Earth, the sky, aliens, inner masters, and the stars. But I don't know how to talk with my mother, father, and brothers.

Oh, Spirit, open me to this part of myself.

~~~

I could no longer live without being straight with my family. I had asked Spirit for help. A few days later, I ran around Southold at six in the morning dropping notes at the doorsteps of my family members. "My house, noon. Please be there. Love, Mike."

On the morning of the talk, I wrote in my diary, "In a way, the very idea of inviting my entire family to my house for me to talk to them is crazy. So is *not* doing it. What the heck."

~~~

Everyone arrived at noon. "What's going on, Michael John?" my father asked as he walked in the door.

Although my heart pounded, I reflexively said, "Oh, nuthin'. I just have some things I want to tell everybody."

They all sat on our large L-shaped sofa. Mom, Dad, Bob, Jackie, Rick, Ellen, Nancy, and Steve, all facing me. All waiting. As I found my way to the piano bench and saw the scene, I flashed back to my first frightening appearance as an attorney before the Appellate Division of the New York Supreme Court. At that time, I thought my entire *life* was on the line. Looking back, those robed judges were a piece of cake compared with the group I faced that day.

"Last week," I started, "someone said to me, 'The higher the monkey climbs a tree, the more you can see his ass.' He was probably right, but I intend to keep climbing. So now I'm letting you all see my ass. I am here so that there is some direct understanding of what's going on."

I was formal, holding the letter I'd written to them a month earlier and various notes on my lap. "Please save your questions and attacks for the end," I said.

I told them about the anger I felt towards some of them. I told them how I had heard Donald Epstein talk about "empowering those around you" and how, when it came to my family, I felt inept at doing that.

Confused and curious faces met me from across the room, as if I was convincing them that I *was* crazy. I continued anyway.

I read my August 30 letter to them, then started to quote from some books that were special to me.

"Put the books and notes down and just tell us what you want to say in your own words," my father said, mirroring in both word and tone what one of the appellate judges had said five years before.

I told them about a few of my experiences over the past year, both at Gates and while on the road, and of the fright I had felt each time I got to see more of myself. I told them about the rebirthing story, of the lightning bolts and the terror-filled screams, and how it ended with "God in the body of the lawyer." No one laughed.

I confessed to Dad, to the extent I could express it, that I had been arguing with and yelling at him for months, and how I had been keeping it in. He denied having thought or spoken the words I attributed to him.

"And family," I said with a tone of both condescension and defensiveness, "don't kid yourselves. I know some of you have made comments that Annie and I are just 'rearranging the furniture,' but there is a big difference between going into a new room and just rearranging the furniture. I believe Annie and I have moved into a new place."

One by one, I acknowledged the fears they might have of taking certain steps into themselves. Then I preached. "All I can say is that the fear is real, but there is nothing on the other side of that door that isn't already on the inside."

"Just don't become complacent where you are," I continued, "and bury yourselves in distractions like houses or cars or office products. I am an expert at this."

Finally I said something like, "I'm dumping all this crap on you because I figure as long as I'm thinking it, I should be honest enough to say it directly. What I'd really love is for all of you to do the same. Any questions?"

"So do you think you're the messiah?" my father asked.

"I just don't understand what you're always *looking* for," my mother said.

My brother Bob, said, "interesting," and walked out.

"I thought my face-to-face self-exposure would touch them." I said to Annie after everyone had left. "I think I convinced them that I'm 'touched, instead.'"

"I think that's what you did," Annie concurred, kindly stemming her "I-told-you-so" in my moment of despair.

~~~

TWENTY

Never consider yourself a failure, you can always serve as a bad example.
—Mrs. Bernie Siegel

LIFE CHANGES, EARTH CHANGES

In the aftermath of my "great" family meeting, hurt feelings, confusion, and self-doubt abounded. Could it have been this way for the early pioneers? Did they need to convince their brothers and sisters and father and mother that it was rational to walk through hostile lands or voyage on deadly seas to get to some elusive Eden? Behind their free-spirited words, were people like Whitman and Thoreau frightened inside that they had left mainstream society? Mainstream *religion*? The questions flowed as from a glacier-fed river.

In my diary, I wrote:

September 29, 1992

Why do I still feel a neo-Christian guilty/fear hook? "If you drop out of your religion, your spiritual progress will be halted." What part of those words is still me? Is such a halt

121

possible? I really don't believe so at this point. Why did I buy into any one teaching or lifestyle in such a big way? Why is my ego so huge viz-a-viz religions and people who cling to them?

Two minutes after I wrote that, I randomly opened Richard Moss' <u>Black Butterfly</u> and read this ("Ask and it shall be given"):

"The acknowledgment of ignorance — that I lack full comprehension of anything — is a sacred act that takes ordinary experience and makes it a door to infinite possibility."

~~~

The questions continued nonetheless, as if *these* were the rivers and mountains and deserts I had to cross, as if my doubts were my Donner Pass, where dozens of early pioneers froze to death and became meals for a few that survived. A trip to New Mexico was easy in 1991. Could I get past this journey through my self?

October 10, 1991
Southold

Dear Diary:
Has anything changed in the past twelve years? Am I still kidding myself that something "spiritual" is happening to me?
I look back at diaries from 1977 and see my great spiritual experiences. Yet the experiences I've had this past year make those seem insignificant, as if the early ones were minute glimpses.

Are they all minute glimpses, even the lightning-through-the-chest electricity? Altar of God, White Lights. All just "peeks"? Are these experiences just sideshows to the grandeur of BE-INGNESS?

Am I as "awake" as I feel I am? Am I so much more aware than everyone around me?

And a few days later:

October 14, 1991

Busy, busy mind. It's driving me crazy. After several busy hours in bed in the middle of the night, I finally repeated, "BE HERE NOW" to myself over and over again.

I feel so very "brainy" now and lately. So much mind trying to run the show. It could burn a body out—literally. I'm pretty burnt right now, but my mind is humming and whistling away at Mach seven-super high speed.

I need, I want, <u>heart</u> food, not mind fodder.

~~~

Sometimes, I believe, people need a shaking or a flood of inspiration to get past the stuck patterns of the mind. My dreams began to respond to my cries for freedom.

October 22, 1991
Southold

Strange, almost apocalyptic dream.

Annie and I are at a restaurant high up in the Catskill mountains. As we walk down the entrance road, we find it muddy and crowded with people. It is so packed that a large, lime green rescue vehicle has crushed several people on the road and cannot drive forward or backward without killing more.

Two nights later,

October 25, 1991

Dream, vivid beyond vivid.
I'm playing basketball with a stranger at our Earl Street house. The earth shakes! A tremor. I could <u>feel</u> it in the dream. It stops. I go to do a lay-up and the hoop is now lower than I am; the <u>earth</u> has moved!
A three-foot-wide rift suddenly runs exactly north-south between our house and the neighbor's. Then the ground rises. It pushes up the ground on the east side of the split.
As I observe the large rift, which looks like the San Andreas Fault, one, then two white-and-red planes fly over the split. In the dream, I guess that they are taking news footage. As soon as they pass and I walk towards my front door, the sky turns instantly from light to dark.
Still in the dream, I know that this tremor was just a prelude to the big one, so Annie and I pack essentials in the motor home to head toward Harriman State Park in upstate New York.

I shared these dreams and visions with Annie, but breathed not a word to anyone else. If I had acted strange or weird up to that point, anyone who knew what I did next would have had me locked up.

Upon waking from that last in a series of dreams of earth changes, I actually spent the afternoon packing the motor home. We had planned a visit to friends up in Vermont, anyway. But in addition to packing what we would need for that three- or four-day trip, I packed "essentials" for the long haul: tools, batteries, food, and clothes. As I stuffed extra crackers, blankets, and cans of food into the cabinets, even *I* thought it was crazy.

I wrote in my journal the following night that I realized how my vivid, recorded dreams could one day be "profound or prophetic," how they might show that I had learned to read my feelings more accurately . . . or that I was completely wacked out.

The feelings that week said, "Big catastrophe coming to East Coast of U.S." Specifically, I felt it would happen the weekend of October 25 through 28. I hoped I was wrong.

While I had played basketball the night before in my dream, I was not thinking about an earthquake before I had gone to bed. So the spontaneous aspect of the dream just added strength to my prediction.

But there was more to my strange actions than the fact of having had and felt the visions. I knew from my spiritual studies that dreams were, in fact, rarely literal, and that the symbols were often very personal. But that week, I actually felt *fear* during and after the dreams. I became nervous about the coming year, and about the chaos that would follow such a drastic change.

That fear led in turn to my becoming scared about my own thoughts about self-sufficient housing and stockpiling fuel and food. Would I channel my energy into mere survival and sacrifice love and service for the whole?

I wondered if I would give my life to the greater good, or scramble like a rat for a little turf and scraps of food. It frightened me that I might become a survivor among survivors in a place where love had been forsaken. I would rather die in the flood.

If I accurately doubted my sanity after packing the motor home for survival, what was I to think *after* the weekend of October 28?

~~~

We went to Vermont. We enjoyed a nice visit with our friends Harold and Cathy. The weather up in Burlington was cool and gray, hardly noteworthy for Vermont in October.

Cathy made pancakes on the morning of our last day. We left later than planned. "Let's not take the New London Ferry like we always do, Annie said after we left their home in Vermont.

"Home come?" I asked.

"Because I just don't feel like riding the ferry today," Annie answered. "And we always go that way."

"OK." I said. "Let's go down the Northway past the Adirondacks then get on the New York State Thruway." And it was done. Two seasoned travelers, unchained by time constraints, had made an impromptu decision and changed course midstream.

As we approached New York City, I turned on the car radio to check the traffic report. ". . . Severe winds and record high tides and flooding have hit Eastern Long Island and the Connecticut shoreline," the reporter said. Annie looked at me in amazement.

The News Radio 88 report continued: "The Port Jefferson and New London Ferries are closed—we repeat, *closed*—due to high seas pushed by this powerful, unpredicted storm two hundred miles off shore. Twenty-nine houses have been washed off the South Shore of Long Island by this fierce storm."

Chills ran up my spine. Annie and I sat in the front of our motor home with wide eyes and dropped jaws. Annie had learned to trust my visions, and I hers, but this was incredible. And *this* was no dream!

When we arrived back in Southold, my visions had manifested: the water had risen so high over the road near our house that we had to turn around and take a different route to get there.

Before the storm, I questioned myself. After it hit, I felt my visions were somehow confirmed. Inside, the flooding felt like a prelude to "big ones." Part of me felt like running to tell my mother and father and siblings about what had happened. I didn't dare.

Funny. While Annie and I spent the weekend in Vermont, friends had attended an Eckankar seminar. There, I was told, Sri Harold Klemp, the Living Eck Master, had said something like, "Armageddon is not coming" and he advised people to "keep living day to day."

In spite of what had just happened, I knew he was right. I did not think "Judgment Day" was coming. But I did see certain areas (New York City, for one) as no longer being fit for living. And the advice to keep living day to day was an essential reminder. There was no point in running around reacting to fear of change like Chicken Little, waiting for the sky to fall.

~~~

TWENTY-ONE

Without . . . striving [for things or abundance], many feel lost and directionless.
—Wayne Dyer, *You'll See It When You Believe It*

JOURNEYING IN ONE PLACE

The year 1991 had been a year of incredible travel and adventure for Annie, Kate, Andrew, and me. Between January and October of that year, we had logged twenty-five thousand miles in the motor home. For months after that, we stayed on Long Island, living as normal a lifestyle as we could, earning the "living" people repeatedly said everybody had to earn, and dreaming and wondering and thinking about moving West.

Although we stayed put on eastern Long Island for what felt like an eternity from October through December of 1991, the real journey never stopped. Staying in one place that long also allowed me to see things otherwise invisible to the constant traveler.

November 11, 1991

Awakenings. I wanted to say "Little Awakenings" but who's to judge? I realized yesterday that each time I gave my brother or father or anyone else a "great" book, I was trying to fix them.

Then I realized that they were not broken. The planet is not broken, either. I don't need to fix anything or anybody, even myself. The best thing I can do is just be. Learn to be, Michael. In being, I can resonate in tune with Spirit. I can be a natural Pied Piper.

I am glad that I work in the law office now less than ten hours per week. Yet even this seems wrong. After all this time and all the deaths and re-births of this past year, I can no longer justify being in the lawyer business.

It is no longer difficult or stressful or controlling . . . it's just wrong for me.

November 13, 1991
Southold

New Mexico visions. A strong, strong, clear pull. A high feeling, almost as if a far-off star that is my true home is calling. The star glows inside me.

Not all of my journal entries involved visions, fears, or wisdom. On the morning of November 15, I woke up with the symptoms of a strong "cold." I felt achy and stuffy and wanted to stay in bed. At 7:30 that morning I wrote:

Kate and Andrew just came into my room saying, "Here, Daddy, bed in breakfast." On a tray, they brought me a peanut butter sandwich, a glass of ginger ale, and a jar of olives. Life is sweet.

A few days later, things started moving again.

Saturday, November 23, 1991

Printed the first draft of Flight Lessons on my new laser printer today.
Annie and I are on a "roll" again. Talking about selling the office—the last anchor. Looking at Albuquerque real estate magazines.

Thursday, November 28, 1991
Thanksgiving Day

After finishing turkey, stuffing, sweet potatoes, creamed onions, spinach, corn, and rolls with Annie's family, we drove back eighty miles back to Southold for a visit with the Halls.

"I get along fine with your family, Annie," I said on the drive. "But I feel like a failure when it comes to mine. I feel like it is time to admit that I don't have a deep relationship with any of them."

"What good would that do," Annie asked. "You've already made a fool out of yourself with them."

"I don't know," I said. "I just feel so weird, like when it's time to admit to an old friend that the relationship is over."

"Do you think it's possible for anyone to do that with their own family?" Annie asked me.

"I don't know," I said. "I just feel weird."

The day after Thanksgiving, I represented two clients in court. The fear, anxiety, challenge, and emotion that had plagued me during ten years of law practice were gone. In their place, an even stronger feeling remained: each act I performed as an attorney felt dishonoring to myself and to God. Rationally, I knew that was silly; many ethical men and women practice law. Yet the feeling in me was clear, not ambiguous in the least. I had no place in a law office.

The time had come to stop working for money . . . completely. Doing it a little or "part time," as I did at that time, felt no more true than doing it full time. My journal entries read more bluntly than "not true."

Friday, November 29, 1991

My heart aches. I hurt.

As I practice law and covet each dollar earned, I feel like a whore (with no disrespect meant toward prostitutes). And I feel that I may truly be going crazy as I remove myself more and more from the "normal" world.

During that interminable stint in New York, I even began to journey into the realm of examining my journal writing.

November 30, 1991

To whom am I writing? I used to think I was writing to the Spirit or the Inner Master, as if it were an entity like an angel. Now I don't pretend that I am writing to another being, or that I am writing to share my insight (or lack thereof). Now, I

131

write to log my journey, so that any who follow may avoid some of the pitfalls.

This entire Pioneer Journal, as well the stories in Flight Lessons, are like a series of "before" pictures. Yet when I wrote them, I thought they were "after" pictures.

At this point on the journey, I acknowledge that there may be no such thing as an "after" picture, that the best to which we can aspire is a "be-ing" picture.

A be-ing picture would capture the subject in a moment of full attention, neither anticipating nor evaluating. The sensitive viewer could spot the difference between, say, a shot of someone washing their car while thinking about the office, and someone just washing their car.

There is a big difference. The former is the stressful schizophrenia in which I have spent most of my life. The latter is the profound state of beingness.

Monday, December 16, 1991
Southold

A new kind of hard time, one that would make most people angry to hear about: No office work to do; no housework to do; not motivated yet to work on book #2; so confused.

It must be so hard for people who retire. They have worked Monday to Friday, nine to five for thirty or forty years and then it just... stops. No "have tos." No routine. No pattern. They are dumped into the place of being fully responsible for their time, and for their every action, for perhaps the first time in their lives.

For me, it is easy when I'm traveling or working on a project, but on days like today, what?

My friend Michael Stern called me from Minneapolis that same day in mid-December. My regular phone conversations with him challenged me to at least move through my thought patterns while my body sat still in New York.

We talked about religions, about life, about "Sugmad's (God's) Dream." I shared with him my frustration with religion in any form.

"There is a reason for the hierarchy model taught in religions," he said. "It reflects life."

"I don't buy it," I said. "There is life, not levels. I believe the 'levels' like heaven, hell, the astral plane, the causal plane, and all the rest just exist because people believe they do."

The conversation moved from there to a discussion on the recent jump from Newtonian to quantum physics. "It sounds as if Science has crossed the Continental Divide," I joked with Michael.

It felt so good to be able to talk this way about such things. Michael was a true friend. He was honest. He listened. And he made sure I listened as well. With Michael, as with no one else in my life (including my own wife), I could move beyond dancing around each other's feelings or reactions.

A few days later, I logged yet another "earth-shift" dream into my diary:

Thursday, December 19, 1991 6:20 A.M.

EARTHQUAKE. A small two inch fault about ten feet long. Then the earth shook. I saw the split grow. Ran into the house to get everybody out. After the quake was over, we heard that most of Long Island had no power, but we did.

Five days later, during a peaceful, less "quake-ridden" moment in our house, I wrote:

Christmas Eve, 1991 9 P.M.

Just tucked my two wonderful children into bed. Read them The Night Before Christmas.

Before that, all the Halls gathered at Nancy and Steve's for dinner and presents. Until yesterday, my heart felt so dark and cold I intended to skip that gathering. But yesterday, love slowly crept its way back into my heart. It started when we all watched Alistair Sim in A Christmas Carol, *the Dickens classic. That story, which Dickens wrote in 1843, was 150 years ahead of its time.*

First Scrooge traveled out of his body, then through time. During his travels, long before modern psychology came into being, he was brought by the first Spirit of Christmas to face his past. Then he saw the future as a possibility, changed by each present choice and action. The profound metamorphic heart opening of Scrooge opened my heart last night.

On Christmas Eve morning, while Annie worked at the rehab and Sara Cooper baby-sat for Kate and Andrew, I received a Reiki radiance treatment from Gayle Marriner.

I had walked into her house in my typical heart-racing just-left-the-office way. After a half hour on the table, I completely left my adrenalin-filled heart and tired body behind. "Body work, body work, hurray for the body workers," the Pleiadians said.

Christmas Day, 1991 5 am

Utter silence in this house
No breeze blows outside.
No birds chirping yet.
Not a sound.
Yet my ears ring, my body hums, this Christmas morning.

TWENTY-TWO

Culture shock is unavoidable as you begin to awaken to our presence as well as your own. Your true identity will be a news flash to your third-dimensional consciousness. The impact of recognizing your multidimensional nature will send ripples of apprehension through your limited sense of self, giving the prospect of a sudden, underfinanced move to Calcutta [or New Mexico] far greater appeal.

Mission Control and Diana Lappi,
E.T. 101—The Cosmic Instruction Manual

MASHED POTATOES

On New Year's Eve, 1991, Annie said to me that hell was wherever people said "if only," waiting for outer circumstances to change before committing to something. Then, true to her own words, she said, "I want to move West this summer." After two years of dreaming and planning, Annie was ready to set a date. I was still scared.

In spite of all the traveling, visions, scouting, and soul-searching, I could not come up with any logical reason for our move. Yet at the same time, I could feel not only a pull to be there, but by then I could actually picture the mesa where our house would sit. I could *see* the house, the hill, even the view from the front yard.

"You know what, Annie," I said to her. "I feel like Richard Dreyfus in *Close Encounters of the Third Kind*. Remember? First the spaceship "beamed" him with light as he sat in his truck at the railroad crossing. They encoded him with a picture, but he had no idea what was going on."

"I remember," Annie said. "That's when he started making a mountain on his dinner plate out of mashed potatoes."

"Yeah. And when he finally realized what the picture was, he gave up his family and his job to get to the mountain he visualized." I said. And he didn't even know what it was all about until after he had arrived at his destination."

"He almost got arrested and killed on the way there," Annie added. "Maybe we're like him. Do you think we've been encoded with a message?"

"I have no idea," I said. "But planning our move away from two successful careers to an unknown, far-off world for no reasons is probably looks like building mountains out of mashed potatoes."

I thought about Richard Dreyfus's troubles—his wife left him, his children and neighbors thought he had lost his marbles—which had begun immediately after his encounter with the aliens. Then I looked at some of our own heartaches since we had followed that first "nudge" to travel to Arizona in 1989.

"Maybe some government agency should issue a warning label for consciousness," I said, "the way they do for cigarette smoking and for alcohol and pregnant women: *WARNING: Waking up to a new level of awareness may cause great pain and anguish and result in strange behavior—do not watch this movie, read this book, or listen to these words unless you are willing to go through the pain of awakening.*"

The following morning, despite the warning label, I decided I would go to another Transformational Gate. This one was scheduled to take place in New Jersey on January 18 and 19. Annie had to work on the 18th and had no time off coming, so I decided I would go alone and either hire a baby sitter or bring the kids.

Annie called home at lunch time that day, saying, "One of the counselors asked if I'd switch the 18th with her."

I laughed. "Not too subtle, is it," I said. Annie laughed with me.

In light of a sweet confirmation like that, a few days later I wrote:

January 11, 1992
Southold

Things are starting to make sense now. I feel as though I am waking from a deep sleep. The sleep/awake area is still fuzzy, but my "eyes" are adjusting to the morning light.

Complete surrender
No motives
Beingness
Multi-dimensional awareness
Realization
Big stuff, this vocabulary of the new pioneer. Big concepts. Then I heard the words, "Except if you be as little children . . ."
Time to relax and lighten up and surrender.

Then, two weeks after she had made the firm decision to move, Annie spoke to me at bedtime:

"I'm scared about moving West, Michael."

"So am I."

"But we can't stay here," she said.

"I know."

"Suppose we run out of money. Suppose we can't live without your salary. Suppose we don't like it?"

"I'm scared, too, Annie," I said. "But every time we've committed to something in the twelve years since we've met— getting married, finding a free apartment, getting a job, or whatever — the gifts of Spirit have always shown up. Look what happened last week with that woman wanting to switch work days with you."

"I know, but I want to make sure we're doing what Spirit wants, not just us."

I couldn't answer that one. I was as scared as my wife, but that night, I mostly just listened. We hugged for a long time that night.

Though the romantic aspects of our love life chronically ranged from lukewarm to cold, I was grateful at that moment that Annie could be honest about her feelings with me. I acknowledged myself, too, for learning to be accepting of her feelings. While I could not assuage her fears that late night, the fact of our sharing them had brought us closer together than ever before.

~~~

As Annie and I shared our plans with more and more people, few seemed to understand. In their faces, I could see that many of our friends and family had finally given up waiting for me to come back to the "real" world. We probably did look like two once-normal people trying to shape mashed potatoes on their dinner plates.

Then I realized: it is not a matter of "getting it," it is a matter of *doing* it. Those who merely read or study, whether of the Viking explorers, the pioneers of the Old West, or of the frontiers of consciousness, will never understand.

In my exploration, I did not have to look for food, or water, or shelter. For most of my early adult years, I had just looked for success. Then I hurt so badly I started looking for awakening. *True* awakening, not somebody else's account of it.

So my wish and disclosed motive, as I made plans to share my "pioneer's journal" with the public, was that it serve not as one person's tale of the "other side," but as a crude map of one path toward awakening — such as the early mountain men left for the first settlers.

January 14, 1992
My 36th birthday

Annie and I have been up since 4:00 this morning talking and hugging. She asked me what I want for my birthday. I said, "Nothing" and meant *it. That makes me the richest man in the world.*

Then Andrew climbed into bed next to me while Katie went to the kitchen on her own to make me another "bed in breakfast." I am the luckiest man in the world.

On January 20, after Kate, Andy, Annie and I had returned from another Network Transformational Gate, I logged notes for the travelers who might follow:

Transformational? My body feels as if every single cell had been replaced by a new, more alive one. Each molecule in each part of my body is resonating, humming like a piano string, whistling like a flute (actually, more like a piccolo).

During the Gate, I woke up to, then focused on, my previous lack of true commitment to the Highest. After repeating "Let go" many times to myself in an attempt to actually let go, I switched to "Gas or God?" (from the story Harold Klemp told about the man out of gas on a dark, country road. "What do you want," the voice said as he prayed, "Gas, or God?")

So I challenged myself over and over with variations on the question: "Recognition, or God? Success or God? Comfort or God? Bliss or God? God realization or God? Happiness or God? Pleasure or God? Safety or God?" and so on.

During Sunday's rebirthing class and my last two clear-outs, this focus elevated me to new states of awakening, of being, of dedication.

I learned about myself this weekend, and, in turn, about other people. I was able to suspend judgment of them just long enough to wake up to the mirror, to the simple, profound fact that every "negative trait" I see in them is something I need to learn about myself.

TWENTY-THREE

The road home is often more difficult than the way to the Kingdom of God.
—Paul Twitchell, *The Tiger's Fang*

SLIDING OFF THE MOUNTAINTOP

I had found tools, such as the HU chant and transformational weekends like Gates, and had begun to learn how to reach a certain spiritual mountaintop. On the Monday morning after that Gate, every particle that comprised me resonated, vibrated, and felt vital. A new Energy — a balanced, ringing energy — flowed through me. Then I went to the office.

By 9:30 in the morning, I had returned to the old, familiar, tense state. Perhaps my dreams that night reflected my drastic change in consciousness.

January 25, 1992 6:00 A.M.

A night of "jumping" dreams.
First, I jumped off of a huge bridge. A few people ahead of me dove. I just hung off the edge and dropped feet first.

Next, I wore a metal "wing" on my shoulders and was going to jump off a cliff, but I didn't trust the gadget, so I didn't jump. Then I jumped out of a plane with a parachute and skis on.

Same day 9:00 P.M.

A day of "dropping" (emotions)
Started out the day at even keel.
Followed, for the rest of the day and evening, by sadness, anger, and the "blues." It feels like another "death," and a dramatic one.
The Mike Hall, Family Hero didn't just fade away; by changing from lawyer to would-be writer he changed to screw-up/scapegoat as fast as Superman changes to Clark Kent. Breaking away from an old script is not easy, and certainly not filled with extrinsic rewards.

The night that followed that entry, January 26, 1992, is where this book started: when we officially announced our plans to move. First came the shocking and bitter reaction from my father, then, after Annie announced to her family that we would be moving to New Mexico in five months, a tense silence filled our house.

Dreams, I learned that day, rarely stir up emotions; actions do. As long as our move and change of life was just theoretical, friends and family paid little attention. When we announced that we had made specific plans to go, we heard, "What are you going to the stupid desert for?" and "How can you leave your family?" and "What are you running away from?"

The following day, I took Kate and Andrew skiing. We arrived well after dark and parked the motor home in the lot at Shawnee Mountain. I stirred that night. I felt so tired, but I could not sleep. I stirred because my wife and I were planning a two thousand-mile move that made little sense to me and that angered both our families. I also fretted in the motor home that night because I had, weeks before, sent my first manuscript to one of the biggest publishers in the world and was now anticipating a response.

Andy and Kate slept peacefully that same night. They slept soundly because they were not living in the future or in the previous day's conflicts, as I was. They lived and slept soundly with God in a huge, sacred ocean called the Present Moment.

On the night we returned, I wrote:

February 2, 1992

Three days of skiing now over. Spending time with a four-and five-year-old experiencing a big, new world exhausted me more than a dozen runs of fast skiing. Andrew and I both grew this week. I learned to let him go, and he learned to be happy in a strange setting. Andrew challenged me. I also challenged myself.

At one point, I started from the top of the mountain, vowing to dedicate the run to improvement, to reaching a new level of skiing excellence.

I turned toward the fall line. I focused. I concentrated. I was determined. I went twenty feet ... and fell ... hard. Slam! Ouch!

Lesson: Attempts to achieve higher levels may result in painful falls.

My own journey, my commitment to achieve higher levels, brought me toward another hard "fall" this afternoon. I wondered if I had a master anymore, as I believed I had for so many years. I wondered if I had a path at all. Religion and group consciousness can give such comfort, but can they give God-realization? I want God, not group acceptance.

Jesus said something like, "Foxes have holes, birds have nests, but he who dwells in the house of God has no place to call his own."

~~~

TWENTY-FOUR

Nobody, as long as he moves about among the chaotic currents of life, is without trouble.
— Carl Jung

POINT OF DEPARTURE

February had come quickly. June lay four too-short months ahead. Moving time was approaching. The long list of hypothetical questions and issues that had been hanging around for months were swiftly moving into the foreground of our "reality." I discharged many of these in my diary each day.

February 2, 1992
Southold

Where is the pioneer now? Body in Southold, Long Island, New York. Mind scattered all over: law office, skiing, New Mexico, a series of books, marketing the first book.
Scattered mind.
Today Katie said, "Daddy, your aura looks pink. It's not black anymore."
I'm glad she saw it, and I'm glad she said it.
So where is the "pioneer" now?

Still willing to give up everything to head West?

Actually, feeling nervous. A little scared about living on a low income.

A little confused about why I'm doing any of this. Why law. Why quit law. Why write books. Why ask all these questions? Why do I analyze (or, as Don Epstein says, "anal-eyes") so much?

The pioneer journey is about the move to enlightened living, not just enlightenment. And I need not be so concerned about the parts of the journal not yet written because this is to be a diary of the journey, not a planned overview of it.

So the phase of the journey I am in now is called "committed to making the trip but having second thoughts about the decision." It is part of the journey.

Do I really want to give up a job where I can work ten hours a week and make a hundred dollars an hour in exchange for the unknown? (Yes)

Do I really want to move away from this lovely, friendly, temperate town of Southold and go to a city where we know only one person? (Yes)

Do I really want to live two thousand miles from my family and my in-laws?

Am I sacrificing something "real" for an ideal?

I know it does not matter where we reside, yet I feel, and Annie feels, too, that it is time for us to move to the Southwest.

To move for moving's sake.

To change for change's sake.

To travel for travel's sake.

While I am not a bird,

I am not a tree, either.

I choose to live mobile-ly

To be free to flow with

The wind of Spirit

I had thought the "point of departure" was where we said goodbye to family and friends. But it lay closer than that; the point of departure was where my old, comfortable, static ideas ended and newer ones became fully free to enter. This was the point of departure, the swirling beginning of the yellow brick road, the road home.

February 3, 1992 7 A.M.

I originally conceived this journal as telling the story of our move from A to B, from New York to New Mexico, from social consciousness to higher consciousness.

Now I don't think that is possible. The "A" part is fairly easy— if I can be honest about the so-called starting point. But the "B" part does not exist. There is no end, no termination to this expedition. Though a big part of me would really like it, this book cannot have a "happily ever after" chapter. The journey is the story, not some beautiful, mountainous land, or some mythical heaven. Not even a state of enlightenment.

Fourteen hours later . . .

February 3, 9 P.M.

I'm scared of actually moving to New Mexico, scared of living in a new house in new neighborhood. And what about schools?

I'm glad I am feeling, even if the feeling is fear, rather than masking or covering feelings with business, or busy-ness or any other distractions.

To feel is to be alive. To hide or deny feelings is to live a living death. I would rather live and feel and face those feelings. As feelings come up, I will feel them, embrace them, and watch them fade like the evening sun.

Big steps taken on this pioneer journey.

TWENTY-FIVE

February 4, 1992

New commitment to Spirit
To God.
The ocean before me
The road behind me

I stand, frozen,
before taking the leap
The hills and bumps of that road
prepared me for this step
into the ocean of love and mercy.
I'll leave my sore heart
on the threshold,
leave anger there, too;
An empty vessel to float
And to fill with love

The ocean before me
The long road behind
A dolphin am I now
A mer-man
The long road behind
on this pioneer journey.

The long road behind
has left me weary
I offer life my heart
It is time.

HELL REVISITED: EMOTIONAL WINTER

If February had arrived quickly, somehow the clock had slowed during that dreary, cold winter month on Long Island. The reality of the upcoming move brought a tension to my chest that would not go away. "Anticipation is better than realization" my father always said. Nothing could have been further from the truth. As I continued to look at my life, at both the cycles with Annie and the coming farewells with people with whom we had been close for thirty-five years, I could only anticipate loneliness, fear, and parting. I lived in my diary those weeks:

February 6, 1992 4:15 A.M.

I'm "nervous" today. Apprehensive. About nothing.

I keep thinking the phone is going to ring and it's going to be the editor at Penguin saying they want to publish Flight Lessons. But I don't feel excited. I'm making fresh pizza tonight. I just vacuumed all the carpets and brought in our sheets and pillowcases off the line. Fun.

So why is my chest tight? I only have two active files in the office. Both are fairly smooth now.

Why am I nervous? Am I a big phony like the TV evangelists? Is that what I'm afraid of?

I don't know.

What I *did* know at that point in the journey was that a series of confrontations lay on the road ahead.

February 8, 1992 9 A.M.

Again today I feel that "non-specific anxiety." I feel tense, nervous, like there's an impending conflict/discord.
Just feeling this way is a bigger challenge than going for a goal.

February 10, 1992
Southold

Anger — intense, raging anger.
But . . . the anger is a mask. Just under its pulsing black and red shield, is a child in need of sobbing. Deep sadness over my relationship with Annie . . . or the lack thereof? She has made no attempt to do anything but avoid me. Is this the Field of Dreams or a Bed of Aloneness?
We can talk about moving to New Mexico, which furniture to sell and which to keep. We can talk finances, investing, buying. We can even talk about parenting. What to do about Katie chewing on her cuffs and so on. We are great at those things.
But pillow talk? "I'm so tired," she says as she leans over to give me a peck. "Good night."

February 12, 1992 3 P.M.

I feel lost. I continue to feel goal-less and purpose-less.

I've been just "hanging out" all day. I watched TV with the kids, made homemade pizza (with whole wheat crust), and cleaned the kitchen. Then I fell asleep on my bed looking at a map of Albuquerque.

I feel like I'm stuck in Neverland, drifting. Nothing in my life seems right.

How easy, to have a fifty-week, Monday-to-Friday, nine to five job. Just enough "free" time left to cram in cooking, cleaning, shopping, laundry, and maybe a vacation or two each year. No time to contemplate "life." No time to wonder about my place or purpose here.

No "idle hands." No time, even, to think about choices. Where's the best place for us to live? What's the best thing I can do at this moment? This month? For the next three years? Total freedom of choices is scary, almost overwhelming.

Annie and I have been given a "grant" by life. We're both thirty-five and have enough money to live for several years without working. We can stay here or move to Albuquerque, or China, or Australia. We can work any type of job, anywhere, anytime.

I have the freedom to write full time.

Yet I keep hearing voices criticizing "too much freedom." "What do you do?" they ask. "You can't retire at thirty-five," they insist. Is there such a thing as too much freedom, or have we become totally conditioned in this century to filling every waking second with input from outside and given our real freedom away?

Saturday, February 15   10 P.M.

Wish I were asleep.
I feel like I'm in hell. I feel abandoned

Sunday, February 16, 7 A.M.

I didn't dream last night. I just tossed and turned and fretted. When will I let go? When will I learn?

I talk about being a "pioneer" into new freedom and yet I fall apart when my wife wants to go to sleep early on her night off. If this is a season of the heart, it is a dark, gray one, as the weather has been for so long.

As February dragged on, I thanked God for my diary, for it accepted my words and stories and feelings and foibles unconditionally.

I often thought of the early pioneers trudging over hills and rocks and rivers and mud and desert. Then I would look over the notes of this journey toward who-knows-what and wonder which was worse.

Even after the ides of that dark, cold month had passed, everything seemed to be going wrong.

I did not have to read her diary to see that Annie was really suffering, going through a "Dark Night of Soul" of her own. It had persisted for weeks, like the colds and viruses the kids had that month. She had become angry, sad, and frustrated.

Work had begun to frustrate her. And our home was not a place of nurturing then. She was not getting much rest or sleep at home because Andy and Kate seemed to take turns keeping us up at night for weeks. She was not happy with herself, her husband, her job, or her kids.

At 9:30 at night on February 20, the peace of a sleeping family soothed our troubled home. I sat there in the rare, dim quiet, wondering if I was really a pioneer on some fantastic life journey or just a confused man making something out of nothing.

Earlier that day, I had written down our monthly expenses and our fixed monthly income. We had a lot less to live on than I had thought. Either I would have to sell a lot of books, or Annie and I would have to work. But something felt odd even as the word, "work" appeared in my thoughts. "*Everyone* has to work!" they say.

The rude awakening was that the new life we had planned might not be the permanent vacation we had thought it would be.

Yet I felt more resolved than before that we had to complete what we had set out to do. In spite of my mind's doubts, a deeper part of me— something too deep to get a clear hold on— said, "Yes, you are on the right track, Michael. Don't give up now."

"After winter always comes the spring," I had heard Donald Epstein say when talking about the stages of healing. "Always." I hoped so.

TWENTY-SIX

When you trust in yourself, you believe in the wisdom that created you.
—Wayne Dyer

AFTER WINTER ALWAYS COMES THE SPRING

February 25, 1992 8 P.M.

Today was a big day for the pioneers. Annie, who has been sick and nauseous for four days, has been tight and scared about the move West. This morning in contemplation, she asked "What's best for all life?" She received a single syllable answer: "Trust."

So her lights came on that afternoon, and her new level of trust helped me let go of the obsessive control I had tried to maintain over things. Then Annie got radical.

"Let's put our stuff in storage in Albuquerque and travel all summer," she said. Then, "Let's not get anything but flexible jobs so we can travel as often as possible. Or maybe we can travel full time and home school Katie and Andrew."

"You're making me nervous," I said to her. It amazed me that Annie had made the leap from fear of moving to complete randomness so quickly. "Just yesterday you were saying how scared you were."

"I was, scared, but I know I need to trust more," she said. "I know we can do it."

"But I still like the idea of having a house to come home to after traveling, Annie," I said.

Annie's spark helped the pioneers. I instantly let go of the depressing idea that we would search for jobs right after we arrived. Annie's crazy notion also freed me from my regular scanning for another "nice" house in the Sunday Albuquerque Journal we were getting by mail.

In just a few days, Annie had let go of her tight link to her present job in the rehabilitation hospital (four days of diarrhea had forced that) and simultaneously, her fear of the move. She really wanted to move on.

So on that day we confirmed that June 22, 1992, the day after Katie's last day of kindergarten, would be our firm departure date. I wrote a letter to our landlords telling them we would be out of the house then.

After Annie's leap of consciousness that day, our discussion jumped from rental trucks, to towing cars, storing furniture, when to look for a place in Albuquerque, when to register Kate for school, what pieces of furniture to sell and for how much, and when to have a yard sale.

We were moving West!

~~~

Sometimes little things remind us about the big ones. Three or four pages remained in my diary, and three or four hours remained in February. Little things. But not really. The stories that my spiral journal held were over. The months of dreaming and scouting and fretting a life change that filled its pages were over, too. A new month, a new season, and a new life cycle were obviously, and of necessity, about to begin.

I filled those last few pages with a recap that, though I had lived it, amazed me.

February 28, 1992
Southold, New York

In the past two years— it was two years ago this month that Annie and I flew to Arizona to "check out the West" —we sold our four hundred thousand dollar dream house, moved into a rental house, diminished a busy law practice to nothing, traveled twenty five thousand miles in a motor home, attended five Network Gates, touched the stars, stood at the Altar of God, connected with all life, read many, many great books, wrote two books (if Pioneer Journal counts), received a wonderful letter of praise from a senior editor at Penguin USA (but no publishing commitment as of this writing), left (in heart) the spiritual path I have clung to for eighteen years, then realigned with it from a broader viewpoint.

These past two years have also seen many painful "deaths."
My ego died (several times; it just keeps popping back up), my relationships with my father and mother and brothers died. The relationships that died were dark and sticky. The ones that are reforming are lighter, and a little more real.
Two years have seen Katie grow from know-it-all "I-have-it-all-together" four to know-it-all "I-have-it-all-together" six. She has grown sweet and bright and strong. Andrew has grown

from baby two to Teenage-Mutant-Ninja-Turtle four. His face is as bright and radiant as ever. He soaks up information like a sponge with eyes, yet is still not as overtly "smart" as his big sister (or perhaps not as much in his left brain as she).

Annie and me? Two more years. Flight lessons? We have reached the stratosphere of love, and have crashed in deep, dark canyons of hell. We have bonded, and broken. We have relished and ached. In spite of all the respect I have gained for her, I still spend time away from her with anger boiling.

We have seen and met beings from all over the universe. We have stood at the gateways to heaven and stepped through. Yet we each have so much "baggage"—hurt and unexpressed feelings going back to long before our births—that even our cosmic flights have been tethered.

Annie and I have learned, through books and therapy, about the subtle addiction called co-dependence. Together and individually we have worked on freedom, love, independence, and bonding. But we are certainly and obviously not yet masters of that razor's edge called detachment.

We are more like young teen-agers, thinking they are adults; not emotionally or spiritually seasoned enough to ride rough cycles with grace, but strong enough to get through. When the tough times come, one or both of us tightens to the point of pain. Then the other heart can't get through.

I still wonder where "we" as a couple fit into this journey toward awakening, life, God-service, mastership . . .

Can one enter the heart of God before he has released his heart to another? Before one has learned to love parents and ancestors? Before one has deleted fear or vanity from the forefront?

I don't think so. We are, for each other, mirrors. We are mirrors so accurate we rarely believe that what we see in them is ourselves. We are, for each other, grinding stones, slowly and sometimes painfully, and with sparks flying, honing the other's jagged edges. This is the nature of relationship, and of community.

We are, to each other, masters, teachers of life, love, and feelings. We take turns leading each other from dark to light, from ignorance to awakening (how painful it is to awaken sometimes—how easy to detest the alarm clock!)

We are hand-holders for each other on this big journey. We hold for comfort, balance, guidance, and for love. Sometimes the grip is tighter than at others. Sometimes it is warmer. Like the seasons.

At the beginning of my last notebook a year and a half ago, I wrote that by the end of that diary I would be a "master." Since then I have filled six hundred pages with struggles and travels and woe-is-me sadness. Am I a master? Ha!

Yet the master within is waking up. I am waking up. It is a slow process, like the blooming of the flower. Can't be rushed. Can't be forced.

"Breakfast is ready!" Annie's shouting from the kitchen. Time to go.

A new month had begun. New information was coming in. It was time to get out of bed and move on.

TWENTY-SEVEN

"Wake up, earthling!"
The message I heard.
"Just a little longer . . . please."
My response.

It's the Holy Spirit's job not to respect comfort zones, but to
bust them . . .
—Marianne Williamson, *A Return to Love*

WAKE UP CALL

Sunday, March 1, 1992

Dream. We sat in our neighbor's back yard, Kate, Andy,
Annie, and I. We were petting a friendly, soft lion and a big
dog. The lion looked up toward the sky. I looked up. A huge,
wooden spaceship hovered above us in the sky, giving a threat-
ening vibration. The four of us hid under a canopy.

On March 5, 1992, only three months and ten days remained
before we would actually move, but things were moving.
Having just filled one spiral notebook, I grabbed an empty one
off my bookshelf. For perhaps the first time in my journal-writ-

ing life, instead of chronicling my personal thoughts, actions, and feelings, I wrote in the second person.

March 5, 1992

The message, not my message, not someone else's message. Just "the message:"

Wake up, earthling! You are a God-being who has been asleep for a millennia. You are part of Life!
If you don't listen to this wake up call you will destroy Earth and miss its message.
This message is part of all life. It is in your DNA. It is in your bones. It is in trees and rocks and mountains and rivers. Whales and dolphins broadcast it to you. The wind carries it past your ears.
Listen! Go to a quiet, natural place and LISTEN!
Wake up, Earthling!
Wake up, Michael!

Neither I nor the untouched, blue-lined pages of my new journal could have expected such a radical start. From the scared and emotional tones of a dozen previous diaries, it was suddenly as if I were channeling a message to Earth from someplace else.

I had planned on opening that fresh diary with a cute "review." Something like, "In our last episode . . ."

But I was seeing that urgent "message" everywhere I looked. It needed to be written and shared more, so I wrote it.

In addition to the wake-up stuff, I was getting another message: as spring struggled to bust through the clouds and drizzle of March, love filled the airwaves.

March 6, 1992

LOVE!
Learn about love
Learn to love
Learn to be loved
Return to Love

The cosmic alarm clock, the wake-up bell from Sugmad (God), was ringing. I had always hated it when the alarm woke me up from the cozy comfort of sleep.

"Just ten more minutes in bed, Mom," I had always begged. "Please."

It was the same with this new wake-up call. For some, it is just too painful to be woken up. I felt that pain.

On March 10, I received a Network clear-out from my brother Rick. During the adjustment, I reached peaceful, high states.

Then —*wham*— a few hours later, I felt depressed again. Fast cycle. Feeling sad, angry, frustrated. And hungry.

And at that time, my body had begun changing in ways I could not understand: for no apparent reason and with no conscious effort on my part, I no longer knew what to cook or eat. Foods that had been favorites for most of my life suddenly seemed inedible.

I shared my peculiar feelings with Annie that evening.

"I've been feeling the same way," she said. "First of all, the sun hasn't shone here in six weeks. That's enough to make anyone lose their appetite or feel depressed."

"But what about the food thing?" I asked her. "Do you think it's just because of the gray New England weather that I can't find anything to eat anymore?"

"Could be," she answered.

"It feels different than that," I said.

"Maybe it has something to do with what that Pleiadian article said?"

"What was that?"

"It said something like, 'As your frequency changes you may find yourself not liking food you loved one or two years ago. You become more sensitive to the frequencies of the food.' They even talked about the way animals are slaughtered and how we ingest the fear. Maybe that's what you're feeling."

"Maybe," I said.

~~~

My frequency wasn't the only thing changing. That night, *before* I fell into the dream would, the earth moved. An earthquake of 2.8 on the Richter scale had shaken southern Connecticut and the end of Long Island where we lived. The following day, a fierce storm shook our house more than the earthquake had.

March 11, 1992 8:37 P.M.

The wind roars tonight. Roars, bellows. Rumbles.
Lightning, thunder.

Last night, a real earthquake hit here. Tonight, it's "just" a powerful, howling, wind. Wave after wave of wind crashing all around, like giant waves pounding the shore.
A call home . . . home.
Sometimes the dolphins call.
Or the whales call.
Tonight, the wind calls.

As the wind swirled around my house, thoughts and words swirled around and pounded the shores of my head. A stack of books cluttered my night stand. *A Return to Love, Essence, A Course in Miracles, Return to the Garden, Black Butterfly, The Shariyat -Ki- Sugmad.* Book after book. All true.

Love. Forgiveness. God. Spirit. Essence. Soul.

All there. All true.

They whipped around in my full head like the wind. Much of the previous year had been spent delving into others' words and pictures of consciousness. Winds do bring change. A realization hit me that night as gusts and gales hurled from the black Atlantic pummeled our house: *I don't need to read anymore*, I thought.

"What are you doing with all those books?" Annie asked me.

"I'm taking my training wheels off." I said.

"What?"

"I'm going to read less and do more."

~~~

It was easier to read than to step deeper into the unknown worlds inside me, but I knew that time had come. The following night, I thanked my diary for being there, then asked God for help. In the days that followed, and with the big outer life change approaching fast, I stepped head-first into a new, frightening me.

March 12, 1992

Thoughts build their static charge, until my hand grabs the pen and grounds that charge onto the blank page. Without writing, my mind would overload, my head would explode. "We communicate to others what would be intolerable to bear alone," Edward Abbey wrote.

Now what: Love or hate? Build or destroy? Release or hold? Heart or mind?

My heart wants to scream. My mind works at red line . . . Ahhh!

I am at my wit's end. Time to ask God for help. "Wits' end" is a great jumping-off point.

Goodbye, wits. Please help me love, God.

With the books back on the shelf and time to listen to the cries inside, I began to feel my feelings more each day. It was so much easier when we were cruising around the country in a motor home than sitting in one, familiar place. While sitting, there were no distractions from what was going on inside.

March 13, 1992

Stripped of identity. I was an attorney, a nice, successful young man, a good husband, an Eckist, a Kiwanian. Now I am a nothing. I have no external identity. It's so easy when you have an identity. You fit in the group.

But stripped of the external validations like money, referrals from happy clients, approval of my writing, approval of my success, my world is left empty. Now I must learn to see, feel, recognize and be nothing but essence. Painful shifts.

Spirit fills empty vessels. Spirit uses available beings. I have been filled with sorrowful and self-loathing thoughts for so long, I left no room for Spirit.

Time for another shift.

Just by choosing to look, previously unseen parts of me had come into focus. Each new realization in those weeks felt as if a light had come on in a dank, dark, long-forgotten basement. Like feeling my own lack of identity about which I had written the night of March 13, the initial sight and feeling of all the emotional insects and vermin inside me sent quivers up my spine.

March 15, 1992

Perhaps I am a master after all. I have mastered the "hurt puppy" role. "I'm so hurt 'cause she doesn't love me. I'm so alone. So forgotten."

I've seen this trait in so many other people lately. Didn't see it in myself.

Now I can see it—clearly.

A hurt puppy is focusing on his hurt, his abandonment. Where the attention goes, the energy flows. So I have been creating this situation that has tormented me for so long. And recognition of the pattern-maker is an essential stage in healing.

Now that I see it, what do I do, Spirit?

After I wrote that question, I closed my diary. Then, using a technique I had originally learned in the Eckankar teachings, I flipped open a book at random for an answer. The huge pile of books that had ruled my night table was gone, but *A Return to Love* still sat within reach. The page I happened to open to read, "Spirit: 'Don't try to purify yourself before coming to me. I am the purifier.'"

Could I do that? Could I drop the make-yourself-perfect stuff and accept Spirit's guidance? The following day, I drove to my psychologist's office. The emotional weight of what had recently surfaced, combined with the accelerating, compressing calendar, brought me over the edge.

As I sat on John Klindienst's couch in the middle of a "normal" session, in front of a man my own age with whom I often talked about cars and skiing and had once played racquetball, I cried.

"Silly me," I joked.

"It's OK, Michael," John said, as he handed me a box of tissues. But the tears rolled on. Again and again I tried to smile and joke about a grown man like me sobbing.

"This has been building up for weeks," I cried to John.

"More like years," he said.

"It feels good to let this out," I said to John, "but I feel so weird doing it face to face with you." I did it anyway.

"By finally letting your emotions show with me," John said, "you're beginning to accept yourself as you are instead of trying to be perfect. Perhaps the brave, continent-roving pioneer has taken his first *real* steps into the new world, Michael."

~~~

There was peace in the vulnerable honesty of that new world. At daybreak on the morning after that emotional session, I wrote:

A deep, deep, restful sleep.
A peaceful morning. The sound fills my head, like a high frequency receiver (and transmitter?)
Peace. I thank God for this moment.

~~~

"Mike, my landlord wants me out in two weeks. Can he do that?"

"Mr. Hall, the seller refuses to fix that broken furnace. Please call their lawyer right away."

"Mike, I just got this letter from my insurance company. Can I come right over."

I was so close to being finished with that law practice. So close. With a flurry of phone calls from panic-stricken clients, that peaceful morning had turned into a tough day. The peace could not last. A harsh wake-up call it was, like someone ripping the blankets off or a blaring alarm clock.

I felt tempted to smash the alarm clock to pieces. I had felt such peace just an hour or so before.

It's not something you can hold onto, this enlightenment thing, I thought to myself in the midst of the lawyer's battle-ground. So often I had said, "I've got it!" as if higher awareness were a brass ring. I was learning that it is not that way at all.

~~~

The alarm clock had rung. I had begrudgingly opened my eyes and rolled out of bed. But my breath smelled, my hair was a mess, and I had crust in my eyes. The morning light had revealed parts of me and feelings formerly shrouded in unconsciousness. Then, after I later discovered that enlightenment had an ephemeral nature—that it wasn't a goal—I had to give up yet another layer of my belief system.

As those weeks on Long Island had shown me more of the dark facets of my self, the time after our life plans had become public revealed a panorama of Western culture that suddenly appeared ugly.

TWENTY-EIGHT

"There is a general reality to Life," said Heather.
"Only by agreement," her teacher Alana replied.
—Heather Hughes-Calero, *Woman Between the Wind*

WHITEWASHING THE FENCE or THE BIGGEST CULT OF ALL

Tom appeared on the sidewalk with a bucket and a long-handled brush. He surveyed the fence, and all gladness left him and a deep melancholy settled down upon his spirit. Life to him seemed hollow and existence but a burden.

At this dark and hopeless moment an inspiration burst upon him. Tom Sawyer pretended to like his awful task as his friend Ben walked by.

"Oh come now, you don't mean to let on that you <u>like</u> it?" Ben asked.

"Like it? Does a boy get a chance to whitewash a fence every day?" Tom Sawyer replied.

"Say, Tom, let <u>me</u> whitewash a little," Ben begged Tom, bribing him with his apple for the "privilege."
—Mark Twain, *Tom Sawyer*

~~~

I had thought of Twain's cute story often as I entered my second year of law school in 1980. "If I bust my ass and make

Law Review," most of my classmates would say, "I might get hired by one of the Big Ten."

Making it into one of those firms meant a high starting salary and giving up much more than an apple for the privilege. A few years after graduation, the ones who had become associates in those firms looked pale from seven-day work weeks. Many of those days were so long, they slept in bunk rooms at the office. Yet they believed that they had achieved something great, so they plugged on.

"If I keep working hard for five or six years," they would say (though many had not spent more than a Thanksgiving or Christmas with their families since law school), "I might make partner."

Making "partner" meant earning the chance to whitewash the fence only five or six twelve-hour days a week instead of seven eighteen-hour days. The carrot for such an honor was the partnership title and a salary in excess of two hundred thousand dollars a year.

While such large salaries failed to woo me, I did not see the dark side of the process—the unconsciousness of it—until after my journeys. Though I rarely worked more than fifty hours a week and *always* spent Saturdays and Sundays at home, I, too, had spent many of my early years as a lawyer desiring more things and thus working towards higher and higher income levels.

Later, when I realized the shallowness of my task, a deep melancholy had settled upon *my* spirit. Yet an even bigger picture came after that. The frightening recognition that the masses—not just lawyers—were stuck in a similar unconscious rut came when, at the age of 35, I decided to get *out* of the lawyer business. That more universal picture—which inspired me to apply the word "cult"—appeared as our move to New Mexico stood less than three months away.

"What are you running away from?" had not just come from upset family members. Disapproval and anger came even from those who lacked the personal connection our families held. "You're NUTS!" came from the ones who knew how much money I was earning.

"What are you going to *do* all day?" came from young and old alike, as if not to have a job was to do nothing.

"You *can't* retire at your age" came from those who "had" to wait until they were sixty-five. Many who knew of our plans just rolled their eyes.

For some, being told I was not going to play golf all day and that I was writing a book softened their initial horror. Those people just asked, "What are you going to do for a *living*?" There were some exceptions. A friend, Darline Duffy, said, "I'm proud of you and Annie, Michael. You are collecting experiences instead of things." But she was one of the bright spots in a world of dark criticism. Most people attacked.

Behind my reflexive defensiveness, I saw a universal message: "It is *not* OK to leave a successful, respectable enterprise." Then I began wondering where that message had come from. Even for the few who responded favorably to my switch to a traveling life and writing career, the message was the same, only with a slightly gentler cap, ". . . unless you replace it with an equal or better enterprise."

Not OK *with whom?* I wondered. Who made that rule? Who said that anything less than nine to five until you're sixty-five is irresponsible?

Who implanted the work ethic and the 1980s success ethic so deeply in people's heads that they reacted disapprovingly to a thirty-five year-old man staying home keeping house and raising his children when he could be in "business" making money? Why had so many people sold their souls and given up dreams in the face of "That's the way it is"?

Then I became aware of a group of people who actually did not react that way. "Great," they said, "follow your dreams." At first, every member of this very definite minority seemed special to me, as if this group were more open to change, more ready for the "Age of Enlightenment."

But as I became more radical in my belief that *all* limitations existed only because people agreed to them, then even *their* level of stuckness started manifesting.

Whenever I discovered that I was in the company of one of those free-minded people, I felt safe to share one of my more absurd dreams: I told them I wanted to fly.

"You mean in a plane." they'd say.

"No," I'd respond. "I've already done that."

"You mean like sky diving or astral projection or something?"

"No," I'd say. "Fly. You know, like Peter Pan."

"Oh," they'd say. (Their face would say, "This guy's not enlightened, he's a fruitcake.")

For this group, it was OK to leave a job, reverse a family role, "break a mold," as they say. But fly? "You *can't* do *that*. What about *gravity?*"

They had bought gravity, I discovered, the same way the first group had bought nine to five, eleven sick days, and two weeks' paid vacation.

So I had discovered two groups: the big one that doesn't like anyone rocking the boat, and the "open-minded" ones who think it is "cool" to rock that boat . . . but not theirs.

I saw that the power of group agreement had become bigger than seeing intelligent individuals like those young lawyers willing—no, *hungry* — to give up their life to achieve a certain status. Group agreement could keep anyone limited.

Group agreement.

"The earth is flat." That prevented travel. After Columbus had returned with "proof" in the form of captured natives, a new world was opened to millions of people who had never doubted the "truth."

"The human body cannot exceed a four-minute mile." That agreed-upon belief—the belief alone—kept a generation of runners from beating the four-minute mile. As soon as one runner (Roger Bannister, in 1954) broke that "scientifically impossible" barrier, the belief was shattered. Within months, breaking it became the normal course.

Was my desire to fly any different?

"Of *course* it's different," those few who would humor me and continue the conversation would say. "It is scientifically impossible!" After the awesome events of the past year, that logical explanation no longer held any weight. Suppose one person did it, I wondered. (Actually, I later read in one of Deepak Chopra's books that numerous yogis already have.) Suppose the Roger Bannister of fliers buzzed over the audience on Phil Donahue or the six o'clock news. What then?

The believers in gravity, like the believers in the flat earth before them, would face a brutal challenge: They would either have to get religion real fast and say, "That flier was a saint or an angel," or they would have to dismiss it as a trick or an illusion. Anything to hold onto their cherished, deeply invested belief in gravity. Hold, hold. After a while, though, they might get rope burn.

To hold to *their* beliefs, the priests in the Inquisition killed, maimed and tortured non-believers. Today we are much more civilized: If you break the rules of some churches, they merely excommunicate you, and remind you that you'll go to hell.

When Annie and I announced our move, we were "excommunicated." Even some close friends never spoke to us again. "You're always looking for something!" one shouted angrily, as if that quality were bad.

I often thought of Thomas Jefferson, Thomas Edison, Ben Franklin, and other greats. Weren't they always looking for something? But in the Biggest Cult, one is supposed to aspire to a "normal life" and not look beyond. "Because if you go too far (too far could be giving up a good job)," many still believed in 1992, "you will fall over the edge."

The Biggest Cult is the collective consciousness of the times. Unlike little cults, the Biggest Cult does not need religious or political fanaticism to do its damage. In the unconscious acceptance of beliefs that stifle breakthrough and creativity, the Biggest Cult imprisons the soul of mankind.

~~~

Once one person breaks free of a cult (a belief, an abusive family, the mafia, or world consciousness), all is changed forever. "Commit to your own healing and free everyone," Donald Epstein said. So Annie and I, in the face of criticism and loss of friends, continued with our planned journey.

TWENTY-NINE

*And if only we arrange our life in accordance with the
principle which tells us that we must always trust in the
difficult, then what now appears as the most alien will become
our most intimate and trusted experience.*

*Perhaps all the dragons in our lives are princesses who are
only waiting to see us act, just once, with beauty and courage.*
—Rainer Maria Rilke

THE PIANO

As March drew to a close and we once again prepared for life
on the move, the philosophical entries in my journal suddenly
had to share equal space with the very practical, very concrete
physical aspects of our journey. At nine at night on March 25,
1992 I wrote:

*Is this still a pioneer's journal? You bet it is. Both the inner
and outer journeys are in full swing:*

*1. Each day, I feel more. As I contemplate, the sound current
swirls in and around my entire being. Every cell is coming
alive. As I study A Return to Love, or the Eckankar Discourses
or a channeled lecture by the Pleiadians, I am beginning to feel
the words and their meaning.*

*2. The "real" (ha-ha) journey looms only eleven weeks away.
Yesterday Annie packed the first of several boxes of books.
Today I did the same.*

In just eleven weeks, we'll be loading up a rented truck, hooking up our Hondas behind that truck and the motor home and heading west on Interstate 80.

~~~

Lightening the Load.

Before the journey, literal or figurative, could begin, we needed to lighten our load. We had started back in 1990, right after we contracted to sell our big house on Anchor Lane in Southold.

We took the seats out of our Plymouth Voyager and filled it seven or eight times with junk for the dump. We gave away whatever people would take. Then we put a pile out on the side of the road big enough to fill a pickup truck. Before the garbage men had a chance to collect it, most was picked up by passing "treasure" hunters.

That was just the beginning. As we contemplated the actual move to New Mexico, we unloaded all nonessential physical possessions piece by piece: a bed, a bunk bed, crib, changing tables, sofa, and bicycles. There remained one more possession:the least portable of them all . . .

March 29, 1992
The Piano

Today we sold the piano. I have played that piano since I was in third grade. I cried. I left the house when the movers came over to pick it up because I didn't want them to see me cry.

Great quotes. Great philosophy. Great concepts, these "moving on" and "letting go" and "lightening the load" are. But lightening the load of our five-hundred-pound piano added five thousand to my heart.

When Bob and Rick and Nancy and I were little, before we had each reached six, we took turns picking out songs by ear and playing countless hours of "Heart and Soul" on a clunky old baby grand my father had brought home when I was a baby.

As the musical talents of their children grew, my parents decided we needed a better piano. I was home for lunch the day the new piano arrived from Macy's. I was always home for lunch. Mom used to pick me up from the front of school and race home so we wouldn't miss "Jeopardy." We would watch and answer the questions, and eat fried Taylor Ham sandwiches on white bread with mustard.

One day, as Art Fleming was thanking Don Pardo for introducing the next "Jeopardy" contestant, a big truck backed into our driveway at 43 Earl Street in Carle Place. I was in third grade then. Two strong men brought the shiny new console piano through our front door and into the den.

A few months later, I sat practicing the scales and songs Mr. Wickey had taught me. In fifth grade, I switched to Mr. Beebe, the same man who taught us to sing "Sweet Betsy from Pike" in school.

It is amazing how those memories attach to a mass-produced box of wood and steel and wire, but even the man who came twice a year to tune the piano sticks in my mind more as a family friend than as a hired technician.

In college, I spent hours in the white-acoustic, tile-walled practice rooms pounding away at Steinway uprights and occasionally sneaking into a concert hall to steal a few blissful moments at a Steinway grand. But returning home for breaks brought me to the familiar feel and tone of my intimate friend.

After college, I moved back into Mom and Dad's house while I attended law school. I built a loft upstairs and promptly moved the piano into my newly built suite. A year and a half later, I moved into a caretaker's apartment on an estate. The piano followed me there. When Annie and I were married, Mom said it was our wedding present.

Another couple of years later, the handyman's special house in Southold became its new home. Our cats, Fats and Chuckwagon, would take turns sitting on my lap as I played. Then on to the "dream house" on the hill where Kate, age thirty-six hours, sat on my lap pounding the keys as we sat on the twenty-five-year-old wobbly bench.

A year or so later, my musical friend followed us to the house on the water, and two years after that to the rental house. The piano that had arrived that spring day in third grade brought its sweet, familiar tone to every place Annie and I set up house, never complaining about our failure to stay in one place.

But Annie and I had committed to a mobile lifestyle, and to unloading everything that we could not quickly and easily move ourselves. We had to be portable. The rest of this story was so hard to tell, I could not even put it into my diary. I bought a Korg digital piano in the fall of 1991, knowing it would serve as the replacement for my old but heavy friend.

Then, as our June departure neared, I began to anguish. Sell the piano? Give it away? If so, to whom? To my mother, for whom it was originally intended but who never played it? To my sister Nancy, who had just begun piano lessons at the age of thirty? Or to brothers Bob or Rick, both of whom had played as many songs on it as I before college? I struggled with the dilemma for months. It amazed me how a musical instrument could "play" out so many different issues. But moving time neared, and we needed money for our new life. A painful decision was made: sell it.

Some dollars are more expensive than others. The several hundred we received for our piano were right up there with the money I had earned as an attorney.

Interestingly, Barbara and John Ebeling, who had bought our big house on the water, bought my piano. I felt some comfort that it would be back in the same spot it held while we had lived there, and that on visits I might occasionally play its keys and hear its characteristic sound. Still, I sobbed as the movers came to take it away, and again as I typed this chapter, remembering twenty-five years and a thousand songs played on that piano.

~~~

THIRTY

*Our deepest fear is not that we are inadequate . . . it is that
we are powerful beyond measure.*
—Marianne Williamson, *A Return to Love*

MALCONTENTS OR VISIONARIES

Time began to move faster each day. On April 2, a decision
Annie and I made instantly pushed our June 22 move date to
May 30—for me, anyway.

After having spent the day before looking at rental trucks, we
decided we would pick up a truck on May 30. I would then
drive to New Mexico myself, towing a car behind and place
our diminishing list of possessions in storage. Then I would fly
(the early pioneers couldn't do that) back to New York and hop
in the motor home with Annie and kids on June 22 and go.

After that decision, suddenly less then sixty days remained to
finish a list of personal, family, and business tasks that seemed
endless. Looking forward frightened me. So the day after we
had made that time-crunching decision, I sat with my pen and
journal and looked back:

April 3, 1992 2 A.M.

*Why did those early pioneers leave the flush toilets and
running water of the East Coast to live (live, or toil?) in a mud
hut on the prairie?*

A hundred years have passed since that filthy, proud, pioneer family posed for the picture that wound up in my elementary school textbook. A hundred years.

In the past two years, my wife and I have given up practically everything <u>but</u> running water: a house with five bedrooms, three baths, central air, a brick fireplace, and cold water and crushed ice in the door of the refrigerator. We gave that up two years ago as part of a plan.

Since that time, I have left a busy law practice that earned almost five times the national per-capita income, and let a beloved musical instrument be carried out my front door. Now Annie and I are talking about building a solar house in the high desert of New Mexico . . . out of mud and old tires!

I am sure that if we commence the project, we will look as dirty, dusty and grimy as the homesteaders in that textbook photo. I can also hear the folks back on the East Coast saying, "What the hell are they doing there?" and "Why do you suppose they left this wonderful life on the East Coast?"

Yet the vision pulls me, pulls Annie. A house of Earth in a place of the Earth. A house that soaks up and stores the sun's abundant heat. A house whose only source of electricity is the sun. No waste of fuels. No hook up to the power grid. And a life in the Rocky Mountain wonderland that no well-to-do New Yorker could live or fathom.

Were Annie and I visionaries? Two days later, I logged visions of spaceships again.

April 5, 1992 4 A.M.
Dreams.

Flying at will. I landed on high ledge and waited for an alien ship (with a helicopter-like blade!) to pick me up.

Then I saw another alien ship, then one shaped more like this:

Then, through the lens of a still camera, I saw what looked like two moons in the background, until one approached right over us.

Forty-six days to go.

April 14, 1992
Southold

Pieces falling into place. The office. The rental truck. My plane ticket back from New Mexico to Long Island. The motor home. All is ready.

Things fall if you let them. They fall into place like snowflakes. Like leaves. Like raindrops.

Things fall into place if you let them.

Letting anything fall into place is difficult when one like me has tried to control everything all his life. With a month and a half left and Annie doing most of the packing, I didn't know what to do with myself. I just puttered around. Visited friends. Visited my mother and my sister.

On April 15, the kids and I built a shoe rack for the motor home. Later, we cooked veggie burgers on the barbecue for dinner.

That in-between time was so hard. I felt completely powerless. Not powerless and frustrated, just powerless. Like a teenager without his driver's license. Like a brain without a body. A body without a brain. A body without direction.

I thought of my unpublished first book. And the second book. Were they pipe dreams? Were they distractions from deep feelings? Or were they acts of love and service? I could not be sure if they were my way of being a "co-worker with God," or if they were something else.

"The love of the Sugmad . . . must show itself in deeds of charity, mercy, and self-sacrifice, and not merely in words." From the *Shariyat-Ki-Sugmad, Book Two*.

Thirty-two days.

The process of "cleaning house" involved preparing our rental house for its return to its owners. On April 28, before Kate's school bus would pass by, I jotted the important plans for the day:

April 28, 1992 7 A.M.

A sunny morning. The pioneer father and his son will go to the dump today. Then we'll buy a new toilet seat in Riverhead. Before either of those two adventures, we will drop Kate off at school, then meet a client at the office.

~~~

After appointments and toilet seat repairs and barbecues, Annie and I talked. "I feel so sad. I feel like I'm not ready for the new world yet and I no longer fit in the old one," I said to Annie as April ended. "I mean, do you think this is the tunnel the mystics tell about, the one they go through before reaching the plane beyond the mental worlds?"

"How am *I* supposed to know?" Annie asked.

"I feel like I'm starting to get a perspective on just how vast the mental, causal, and astral worlds are," I said. "You know how the article from the Pleiades seems so accurate and so broad in scope?"

"Yeah, so?."

"But it still just referred to matter, energy, space, and time. We know that there's more than that now."

"What's really bothering you?" my counselor-trained wife asked astutely. I wondered how she knew I was philosophizing to avoid feeling.

"This afternoon, Kate and Andrew and I walked over to the Southold school grounds to fly a kite," I said. "My mother drove by. I know she saw us, 'cause she beeped and waved, but she didn't stop."

"Maybe she was busy," Annie said.

"But we're leaving in a month," I cried. "Wouldn't you think she would want to spend some time with us?"

"You haven't been very nice to your family, you know." Annie said, dumping the situation back on me. "You're not even being honest with your mother and father about your feelings right now."

"What are you talking about," I blurted defensively, even though I knew she was right.

"You should be telling your mother how you felt as she drove by, not me."

"Yeah, maybe," I conceded. "But after my fiasco family meeting last fall, I'd rather do a stand-up routine naked in

Carnegie Hall than to sit and share my feelings with my parents. I feel like they've forsaken me."

"You are not forsaken," Annie said. "Your father bought you a birthday present this year. That's his way of communicating his feelings to you. And Bobby named his son after you and got married on your birthday. They have a deep love and respect for you, Michael John. They just don't know how to handle what's going in your life now."

That night, after writing notes about my conversation with Annie, I wrote:

We know we are moving into a void even greater than the confusing transitory state we reside in now. We both admit we are scared of this unknown future (and the fact that we were leaving not a bad, but a wonderful past). Yet we agreed: we would not have it any other way. "Whatever happens," Annie said to me today, "I would rather take these risks than lead a life of 'quiet desperation.'"
Thank you God, for Annie.

~~~

Twenty-six days to go.

April disappeared in a flash. At 10 P.M. on May 3, 1993, as I sat on the sofa in our box-filled living room, I wrote:

I am crossing over into a world so vast that it dwarfs the universes I have been wrapped up in for this past year. I feel the peace and power of this new place and the need to submit to Spirit's will.

We have seen beyond the little clearing in the forest. We have let go of so many earlier goals and drives that got us to that clearing and nearly convinced us that we need not look any further. Yet it is time to move on.

Now what, Spirit?

The answer to that question came like a deep-woods ambush.

~~~

Earlier that day, during a brief conversation, a close friend had called Annie and me "malcontents."

In a way, he was right. But he did not know why we had chosen to move to the Southwest two years ago. He did not understand what Annie and I were doing or why. "You are looking for greener grass in the wrong place," he said.

When he said that, it hurt, but I knew he didn't know that my wife and I had spent two years learning how to be mobile, light, and even nomadic; that we were consciously becoming "travel masters" like it said on the side of our motor home. Nor did he know the anguish and confusion and self-doubt our plans and journeys had generated.

I had never shared with my friend the "pull" both Annie and I felt to go to New Mexico, or told him of the visions that nudged us to fly out to Arizona in February of 1990. I thought those things were too strange to share.

And because I hadn't shared, he didn't know about all the crying I had done, or about the deaths I had suffered and mourned on the trail.

In our first eleven years together, Annie and I had learned how to: start and run a business, travel, navigate, and to counsel students—even students from violent and radically dysfunctional families. We had practiced communicating with groups, and facing up to "monsters" such as judges and other power figures before whom I, at least, used to tremble.

We had trained for other tasks as well: how to raise and love two unique, powerful, independent children; how to stay committed to a goal and face pain at the same time; how to trust God enough to allow ourselves to cry in the other's arms. I knew the list could go on; it had been an intense eleven years.

We also learned a new set of values. We learned that money and big houses are relatively easy to acquire, yet of no real value.

As the malcontent jab was thrust, I wondered if, in defense, I should tell my friend all those things. Would he want to hear about them or about dreams Annie and I shared when we met? Would the things that convinced me to propose to her back in 1979 sound silly?

Annie and I had committed out lives to God-service before we were married, before we knew what the phrase meant. And I knew that the years that followed had provided invaluable training for whatever mission awaited us. Could I say that to my critical friend? No. All *that* went into my diary. A year later, some would become public in *Flight Lessons* and *Pioneer Journal*. But that day, in spite of my training and practice, I just wasn't ready.

Were my wife and I malcontents? I didn't believe it for a second. But I needed to learn compassion for our detractors. How could they give support to something they saw as misguided (at best) or crazy? And the issue was even tougher for our parents: how could they support what they saw as the demise of their own children and grandchildren?

~~~

In my diary that night I wrote:

May 3, 1992

This world was built by dreamers . . .
Galileo dreamed . . . DaVinci . . . Columbus dreamed . . . the
Pilgrims dreamed . . . Lewis and Clark . . . Franklin . . .
Jefferson . . . Bell . . .
The physical world has been "mastered" at this point in
history because of those dreamers, those pioneers. All of them
were malcontents with respect to the wisdom of their day.

But now things on the planet are happening quickly. The new
pioneers must go beyond land masses, ocean depths, or even
distant stars and journey into the "mystical" worlds that have
been kept at a distance for the past several thousand years.

Jesus knew about them. So did Buddha, and Plato, and
William Blake. Mark Twain even knew about them. But they
could only hint. Merely allude. Some people might have been
ready to "believe" in the bigger world taught by these greats—
"In my father's mansion, there are many rooms"—from the
dusty safety of their own lives, from behind the pages of a book.
But few would venture in.

The New Age, in spite of its commercial misuse, is truly upon
us. In the next decade or two, those still clinging to their money
and security and "benefits" (so-called!) will be like passengers
clinging to a sinking ship. Their only chance of true survival
requires a daring leap into icy cold waters. They can only hope
that those who left the ship ahead of them can pluck them from
the shocking unknown and introduce them to life "beyond the
ship" (so to speak).

Annie and I are leaving the ship early, so that we can prepare ourselves and those who follow for the coming changes. So we can share the journey.

The ship may never hit an iceberg or actually sink (Armageddon is a possibility, not a requirement). But still, those who hold to the "safety and comfort" of the vessel will eventually realize the absurdity of their grip.

~~~

Annie and I were leaving the safety and security of a Titanic-strong vessel, and the comfort of a lush, green tree. We were about to blast off from that ship into the blue sky, knowing we would be blown and buffeted by the winds of change and the flow of Spirit. We were not, I knew, moving to New Mexico as a harbor, a landing spot, or a "tree." We were moving toward a new launch pad.

Ten, nine, eight, seven . . . Twenty-seven days. Twenty-six. Twenty-five . . .

~~~

THIRTY-ONE

During the time of the darkest night, act as if morning has already come.

—Marianne Williamson, *A Return to Love* (quoting the *Talmud*)

DARKEST BEFORE THE DAWN

May 5, 1992 8:20 P.M.

"The only healing is a return to love," Marianne Williamson wrote. Part of the process—for me at least—is to honestly feel and confront (accept) the non-love. Ouch!

Before this pioneer heads West, he wants some kind of "healing" in his relationship with Dad, Mom, and brothers Bob and Rick. But the feeling —the acute, sharp, deep, sadness and hurt and anger— is stealing the limelight right now.

It's ironic: I'm the one moving two thousand miles away, yet I feel so abandoned. I feel deep hurt and resentment for being ignored and unappreciated and even unwanted. And I want to feel love.

This traveler's heart aches. Not because I am leaving in three weeks, but because I do not feel love for my birth family. And I feel that, as long as I hold back love from anyone because they don't give love to me, I am kidding myself to think I have made any spiritual advancement.

~~~

Twenty days to go.

Saturday, May 9, 1992

On that day, I logged a strange, little series of occurrences.

9:45 A.M. The power went out about two hours ago. I believe it went out last Saturday at about the same time.

I enjoy the true peace inside a house without a myriad of electrical fields and transformers and transistors and diodes and motors humming.

Last night, at 5:45 (Annie usually arrives home from work at 5:20) Katie complained, "When's Mommy gonna get home?"

"I'll bet you know the answer," I said, trying to teach her to rely on her inner knowing.

"Six thirty," she said.

When our kitchen clock read six thirty-one, Annie walked in the door.

This morning, the electricity went out. After an hour, Katie asked, "When's the electricity going to come back?"

Again, I challenged, "I bet you know."

"Twenty minutes," she said.

"Let's set the timer," I said.

We set the kitchen timer for twenty minutes. The bell went off. Maybe ten seconds later, the lights came back on. Katie and I looked at each other. I smiled. Katie smiled. I did not have to lecture her or preach about her abilities as soul. She was seeing them for herself.

"It's spring!" I said out loud after that fun morning with Kate, and in a blissful lapse away from self-pity. Spring!

~~~

But even in springtime, it rains. Even in spring, the birds squawk and fight and learn. Flowers bloom, then wither. With tension building each day and a house in pre-move chaos, Annie and I spent days and nights apart. Our distance amplified the emotions that were building as move-out day approached and the good byes had begun .

On May 11, I headed past the potato farms and vineyards to Riverhead, toward what would be my last session with my psychologist and good friend, John Klindienst. In the little hamlet of Peconic, I passed the old Victorian house our friends Dan and Pam Tuthill had restored to a warm work of art. Pam and Dan were our first friends in Southold. It would be a long time before we would see them or visit their home.

I drove through Cutchogue, admiring Punkinville, an old farm where Kate petted her first goat, and Andrew, a deer, and where they both picked their first Halloween pumpkins. As I admired the farm and cherished the memories, I felt emotions building up inside. I knew I would once again cry in John's presence. I continued on.

As I sat in Dr. Klindienst's waiting room, the radio played an Amy Grant song: "Deep in my heart I know the strength is within." Appropriate. A waking dream about the process of leaving and loving. The door opened. A couple walked out, John behind them, coffee mug in hand. "I'll be with you in just a minute," he said to me. The words were so professional. His eyes and smile, which his patients could not see, said, "Hi, buddy. Great to see you."

As I waited, I looked back on three years of sporadic sessions. I had learned a lot in that office. Learned especially about my obsession for resolution, for needing to "finish" one rung of the ladder of life so I could immediately (if not sooner) grasp the next rung. I lived like a zealous Boy Scout obsessively checking off merit badges on his way toward Eagle Scout.

While I still hadn't learned the art of leaving "well enough" alone, I did know better after therapy with John. After Eagle Scout, after one "graduation" would always come another step. "So enjoy the day, " John had reminded me. "Enjoy the process."

I started crying almost as soon as John closed the door behind him. Though we had become much more than doctor/patient in the previous years, John maintained his professional poise that day. "What do you want to talk about in this last session?" John asked me.

"I cry at graduations," I told him. "But this doesn't feel like that. It feels more like I have to start walking through life alone and it hurts." John had become the objective, unconditional ear I had so lacked in the years before our move, and a voice I knew I could rely on. I cried almost the whole hour that day. I felt scared that I could no longer call John up when things got rough and say, "Can you squeeze me in?"

At the end of the session, I wiped my tears, hugged John briefly, and walked out. The "pioneer" had to leave more than his piano behind. The pioneer had to walk out of a place of nurturing and support alone, and walk toward learning where love really comes from. That night, a busy Annie would drive the lesson deep into my heart, as a wooden stake.

May 11, 1992 9 P.M.

I left John's office feeling sad. Arrived home wanting only to be held closely by Annie. She was busy packing. Too busy to comfort me.
Then she went to sleep, leaving me alone again.
I thought the dark night was over, yet deep sadness with coatings of anger wrung me. Why?

Having asked the question in that dark moment, I flipped Marianne Williamson's book open.

"We are not afraid of the dark within ourselves, so much as we are afraid of the light," I read.

Yet I had *seen* the light, I had *bathed* in it. *Danced* in it. Why, I wondered, did I still dwell in darkness on the near eve of our journey West? Williamson's words had been right on so far. I turned the page.

"Our goal is God. Nothing short of that goal will bring us joy."

Right on again. Perhaps I had forgotten. Then, on the opposite page of her book, on the evening after my last session with John Klindienst, I saw words that lifted the unbearable burden of that dark night from me:

"Psychotherapy guided by the Holy Spirit will certainly have a place. No one can escape from illusions unless he looks at them, for not looking is the way they are protected. The way to heaven is fraught with demons on the side of the road, just as the fairy tale castle is surrounded by dragons."

The following night, my hard-working, evasive wife turned over and went to sleep at 8:30, right after the kids. I still felt sad and alone, and the scene inside our house puzzled me.

Annie had been packing boxes for weeks. Yet the garage overflowed with items for Saturday's yard sale, and the house still looked cluttered with stuff. The quantity amazed me, after two and a half years of unloading. I had thought we had so little.

The early pioneers had to limit their possessions to what might fill a covered wagon. They needed room for two hundred pounds of flour, a hundred fifty pounds of bacon, ten pounds of coffee, twenty pounds of sugar, and ten pounds of salt. We, who could stop at a MacDonald's or Pizza Hut for nearly every meal along the interstate highway, could fill four prairie schooners with our "essentials."

That night, as I sat alone in my house with my bulky possessions and heavy feelings pushing in on me, I knew we had more to unload.

Sixteen days.

May 14, 1992 9 P.M.

Alone in the motor home (in the driveway). Not sad or lonely tonight. Tired from helping Annie set up for Saturday's yard sale. She's been working hard all week. Maybe I need to learn to put thoughts and feelings aside sometimes and just work.

The den is empty. The large living room now just has our green sofa in it, no lamps, no pictures on the wall. No piano.

I'm leaving for New Mexico in two weeks.

I know that many are hoping and praying that we will dislike the place and that we will come running back to (their) "reality" in less than a year.

May 15 2:15 A.M.

I just spent a half hour in the middle of the night helping Annie pack the motor home. Then I washed dishes. She's been up since midnight. The whole time I acted "light" and happy and friendly, as if working with her at two in the morning was fun. We have not spent a moment together in over a week.

She is either an idiot or is just so bent on avoiding intimacy that she has put herself into a whirlwind of activity.

Now I'm back in the motor home. My wife just went back to her bed. Here I sit, five years after writing about us sleeping apart, and the pattern continues.

Of course, I could go back to the bed, as I did four hours ago. This would surely put Annie right to sleep . . . then I would be alone—next to her—writing in this journal.

It was not just time to move West, It was time to learn more about love.

THIRTY-TWO

Everything in the universe, including every part of ourselves, wants love and acceptance. Anything in life that we don't accept will simply make trouble for us until we make peace with it.
—Shakti Guwain, *Return to the Garden*

CLEANING HOUSE

Eight days to go.

On May 22, a client called me at the office. "I just want to wish you well," he said. "My wife and I are really going to miss you." It felt so good. A closing. A resolution. But then a call from another client, one whose file I had worked on for almost four years, brought up difficulties I doubted I could resolve in the four hectic business days remaining in New York.

Then old family problems surfaced. I thought my mother had said we could stay in her driveway in the motor home from our move-out date of May 30 until we would head West in late June. "But I thought you were going to stay at the office," she said on that stressful morning. That situation wasn't insurmountable; we could park the motor home almost anywhere. It just felt bad.

A few minutes after I got off the phone with my mother, I gave into guilt with another family member who wanted a shed I had verbally sold to a woman earlier that same day. If I sold it to family, I knew I would dishonor my agreement with the woman. If I did not, I would have to face more family dislike.

I chickened out. With so few days remaining in New York, I gave in to my fear of more family disapproval.

I felt angry at myself that night for handling the situation so poorly. Then, as I shared the day's tense stories with Annie, she said, "There are no such thing as victims, only volunteers."

"You're right," I said. "But I hate the way I feel about my family. I want to feel love."

"Give yourself a break," she said, "you're just waking up to these feelings. You need some time."

"But I am still so frustrated," I said. "A master would love them."

"It's not something you can do overnight, Michael John," she reminded me. "You know what they say, 'It's a process, not a goal.'" She was right, but I still felt like a victim. And I still felt bad about feeling so bad. It had become painfully obvious that day that all my "issues," all the holes or clouds of my beingness, would follow me to New Mexico if I did not resolve them in New York.

I kept wishing that I had resolved things, but they just kept popping up. *Shit!* I thought. Rather, *Thank you, Spirit, for keeping me on track toward truth.*

As I looked around our house that night, I saw a mess: boxes all around, dusty, dented carpets where tables and a sofa once stood. Toys and dolls and bags and tape and scissors everywhere.

Each room, while nearly empty, still seemed full and cluttered. And it was not just the house. The "house" (consciousness) I was leaving was still cluttered with old stuff, some of which had grown impossible to neatly box and put away.

While only eight days remained on the calendar for our physical move, I knew I still had much to let go of before I had "moved" in consciousness.

I wanted to think that everything was cleaned up and ready to roll, but my messy surroundings and tense heart told a very different story. I opened *Journey of Soul*, by Harold Klemp:

"When a symbol comes in your dream which you don't understand, you might ask someone else what the dream meant. But you are really the final judge and jury of your dreams. You must decide what that dream means to you. How does it tie into a lesson that you need to know right now? Often, the mind garbles dream symbols simply because of one's inability to handle the truth directly."

Yikes. My dream symbols (especially the waking dream ones) were of clutter and dust and marks left even after the pieces were gone.

The move, the "difficulties" with my family, challenged me. I could leave, but the marks of my feelings would remain impressed into me. They tested the commitment to spiritual truth which I so often espoused.

Was I committed, or was I a weak hypocrite?

Five days.

May 25, 1992 4:30 P.M.

As I write this, Annie, Kate, and Andrew are dancing to Anita Baker on the empty blue carpet in the living room.

Boxes are stacked everywhere. Sixty or seventy of them labeled and piled, each carefully packed by the beautiful woman now dancing.

Five more days.

Is all this stuff (I thought we had "let go" of so much) going to fit in a fifteen-foot truck?

Is anyone going to offer to help?

Worries drift in and out.

Then visions of New Mexico's high desert drift in, renewing my resolve that we are on track.

High desert. Hot and sunny. Blue skies. Lightning storms. Mountains all around.

So many unknowns—neighborhoods, money, schools.

So many feelings—scared, excited, unloved. So tired. This process—moving (whether in consciousness or miles)—requires a lot of work. You can't move by sitting still.

You cannot expect others to help you move.

You have to prepare your vehicles.

I can't wait to settle in New Mexico. We've been unsettled here for so long.

Four days.

May 26, 1992 9:00 P.M.

The cutting of the umbilical. For weeks and weeks, I have bemoaned the lack of love from my brothers and parents. Sadness, anger, and depression nearly consumed me.

On the phone that evening, my friend Michael Stern gave a more positive perspective to this experience. "This is your chance to dispel the illusions and learn where love really comes from," he said.

His wife, Sharon, spoke from the extension phone. "This is your chance to start with a nice, clean slate."

I got it. For months I had seen so many "other" people —civil service workers, dependent adult children, etc.,—staying "on the boob," staying dependent on outside sources for their love, protection, and security. I had often thought about the phrase, "making a living" and how many people did not live because they were so busy "making" a living.

When I told people that I had "retired" at the age of thirty-six, they invariably said, "If I won the lottery, I would quit working tomorrow." If not a job, then the lottery. So dependent.

I never saw *myself* as such a dependent one.

But I was.

And that evening, after I saw it, the illusion felt pierced and I felt whole and alive.

If the previous months I mourned over the "death" of my little self, that day the mourning period finally ended. And the painful limbo/unconsciousness that followed each death, once over, made room for an awake, alive, free-standing vehicle for Life. It felt like an umbilical cord was severed. I could breathe. Freedom!

After settling from the elation of that freedom, I wrote, "Is this the end of the Pioneer Journal—a month before our "actual" move West? Maybe this pioneer had to leave home to find the *true* source inside: to find out where *love* really comes from."

"If I ever go looking for my heart's desire," Dorothy said. "I won't look any further than my own backyard." Dorothy didn't say that until she had already *been* to Oz.

There's always more. There's no place like home.

Was that simple realization the goal?

It felt like it was. The next month, I thought naively, could serve as the epilogue to the pioneer journey. Only later would I learn that realization without action means little.

The realization felt like a birth after a long, hard labor. The push through the long, dark tunnel had been painful and confusing. Then—ouch! —out into the bright, cold world.

Ouch! No more warm, dark womb.

Ouch! What is this bright place? You mean I wasn't in heaven all along?

You mean I can live without that cord, that lifeline?

You mean there is joy and fullness in just being, no matter what the outside feedback looks like?

Three days to go.

On May 27, things took an interesting turn.

Last night, after a simple reminder from a friend about where love really comes from, I let go. The very next day, some of my family called to offer help us move Saturday.

~~~

THIRTY-THREE

Honest criticism is hard to take, particularly from a relative, a friend, an acquaintance, or a stranger.
—Franklin P. Jones

THE LAST BATTLE WITH THE HOSTILES

One day.

May 29, 1992
Southold, NY

I am picking up the moving truck in fifteen hours. This will be my last entry in Southold, New York, at least until I return in two weeks to drive the motor home out West with Annie and the kids.

Tomorrow afternoon, I will be heading west on Interstate 80, pulling the blue Honda behind the Budget rental truck. Annie and kids will stay behind in my parents' driveway in the motor home.

Final thoughts: Nervous. Still wondering why we are doing this. Still resolute, but the reasons are unclear.

A little nervous about the "signs." In an Albuquerque Journal that arrived today, the cover story focused on how youth gangs have made their way to the "good" parts of town.

This may may mean: "Stay out of the city!" Stay away from crowds, traffic, man-made noise, electricity. (As I wrote that, it sounded so extreme. Then I wondered if it would seem so strange in ten or twenty years.)

~~~

Moving day! We had planned and agonized, faced friend and foe, and looked within for two years. Finally the day for loading the Budget rent-a-prairie schooner had arrived! The time had come to pack and leave for the Wild West! Yet it was no happy day.

My father arrived just as I pulled up to our house with the rental truck. I realized as he watched me unhitch the car dolly that until that moment, he thought this was all a pipe dream for me and Annie.

Between packing the remnants of twelve years together into a fifteen-foot truck and feeling and fielding a host of hot emotions, moving day allowed no time for me to relax, let alone write. The following day, after I had already put five hours and New York and New Jersey behind me, I shared the saga of moving day with my diary.

Sunday, May 31, about 9 A.M.
Somewhere near Hazelton, Pa., at a truck stop on Interstate 80.
Yesterday. The big "pack-up-the-truck" day. Steve Cagen, Rick Hall and Steve Amzler all helped and worked hard. Without them, I don't think Annie and I could have done it.
Dad came by twice, once in the morning to look at the rental truck, then again late in the day to tell me I was too tired to drive.
"I'll be the judge of that," I snapped at him. "I know when to pull over."

"You know everything, don't you?" he answered.

A quick exchange. On the surface, it was about me driving a truck after a long, hard day, but it was really just two people expressing themselves indirectly. I stood my prideful ground and spoke strongly, but I felt like crying.

As Dad got into his car, he shook his head, almost in disgust, "We're sure different, you and I." I had never seen him look so disappointed in me. Then he said something about him being satisfied with the status quo. "Bob and I were saying you are looking for greener grass the wrong way."

I wanted to say, "I know what I'm doing!" but the time to move—and change—had come. I dropped my tough walls and opened up to him, saying "Do you know the fears and second thoughts I've had about this move!"

I almost cried as I said it, but I held the tears in. I was afraid they might alienate my father even more. I felt as angry at him as I felt sad. My father and I, who had been buddies for the past ten years, had come to verbal blows. A rift as wide as the Grand Canyon had grown between us, and we were shouting at each other from across it. I hated him for that. And I hated myself.

Long after my anger had passed, I saw the bright side: it was the move itself that brought he and Bobby to my house for one of the only times in the two years Annie and I lived there. And it had brought Rick and Steve over to help.

This move is about moving, not about searching. Too many people stay huddled in the dark caves of their consciousness, telling themselves it is the best place to be, never basking in the sun just outside.

The move had brought me into the blazing sun on moving day, and it burned. I could only hope that maybe a tan glow would follow.

I drove and drove and drove all day. At ten o'clock (Central time), I stopped somewhere in Eastern Indiana. Before trying in vain to find a comfortable sleeping position on the hard seat of the truck, I logged that day's portion of the journey across America.

I drove seven hundred miles since 4 A.M. this morning. A hundred fifty years ago, it may have taken the early pioneers two months to make this part of the journey.

I had fun today. Busy in each moment, enjoying trees and people and noticing lush, green mountains that I have visited in my dreams. I listened to truckers talk on their CB radios all day. There is a great deal of camaraderie and respect among these diesel-driving men and women.

Tomorrow I should make it to Minnesota.

On my way to New Mexico, I was to drop off a bed to Michael Stern in Minneapolis. Yet besides the fact that I was carrying all of our worldly possessions to New Mexico, that five hundred-mile side trip to Minnesota had little to do with a mattress or with Michael Stern. For me, it was a return pilgrimage to the Temple of Eck.

Monday, June 1, 1992 6:00 P.M.
Minneapolis, Minnesota

As I left the horrible industrial sections of Ohio, Indiana and Illinois behind and entered Wisconsin, I immediately knew that Annie and I made the right decision to leave the East behind. Until that moment, I wasn't sure.

I arrived in Minneapolis an hour ago. This is the half-way point of the cross-country trek. My friend (and Network chiropractor) Michael Stern just adjusted me. Home again. Peace again.

On the morning of Tuesday, June 2, before Michael and I visited the Temple of Eck, I grabbed *The Secret Life of Waking Dreams*, by Mike Avery, off Michael's shelf and flipped it open at random. The story I opened to told about a jogger who noticed that the snails that died in the road were the ones who got halfway across then turned back. The ones who forged ahead all apparently made it.

His "slimy" little story foretold well of our plans to continue with our planned trip. I opened to another story. The second tale concluded, "The grass *is* greener on the other side of the fence." (The emphasis was in the story.)

My visit that day to the Temple of Eck more than made up for the "empty" feeling of my first visit eleven months earlier. This time, I entered the temple with no preconceived ideas, and, especially, no arrogant attitude. I sat in the sanctuary. This time, another kind of "emptiness" touched me.

As I sat there, I noticed something I had not felt before in the temple or in my life: In that temple was a very definite *lack* of the "positive" charge I had felt in Sedona and Santa Fe and a similar lack of the "negative" charge which I felt in most metropolitan areas. The space felt absolutely neutral, and sacredly so. The silence in that space spoke to me, and I could see in the faces of other visitors that they felt the same message: "You are *soul*! You are *free!*"

And that was all I felt. No religious message blared at me. No pushes or pulls. I left the Temple of Eck that morning in a calm, balanced state, with tears of gratitude in my eyes, ready to move on.

Thursday, June 4, 1992, about 11:30 P.M.
"Motel 6" North Platte, Nebraska.

A hot shower and a clean bed. In November of 1973, I slept in a car at a rest stop in North Platte. I was alone then, too, on my way from Salt Lake City to New York. I woke up shivering in my sleeping bag inside a frosty car. Even my own method of traveling had evolved.

About six hundred more miles to Albuquerque. The "wagon" and its turbo diesel oxen are running well. The driver is tired.

Friday, June 5, 1992
Somewhere near Pikes Peak, Colorado

I listened for endless hours to the CB radio today. "Hey, eastbound," the westbound truckers would ask, "what's it like over your shoulder?"

The radio would then come back with the voice of an east-bounder, "Watch for a broken-down four-wheeler about two miles ahead of you," or "You're looking good all the way to the Mile High."

"'Preciate it," always came back, followed by a similar report on what the eastbound trucker could expect. I realized how truckers traveling in opposite directions give essential infor-mation to each other.

The early mountain men did the same thing without electron-ics: they returned to tell their tales of the West, and provided the only information available for the early pioneers. Now I understand the inflow and outflow of Sugmad's sound, which calls Soul, and shows it the way home.

The traveler must travel back to help those who follow.

As I flipped back through my journal, I saw that I had filled many pages with similar realizations, and I knew that those realizations alone were not enough. I needed to step into that new world, not merely have realizations about it.

I stepped on the gas pedal, heading into a new world . . . and an incredible headwind.

THIRTY-FOUR

Wednesday, August 31, 1853 . . .
It blew so hard last night as to blow our buckets and pans
from under the wagons.
—From the diary of Amelia Stewart Knight, near the end of
her journey on the California Trail.

October 6, 1852 . . . the wind blew so heavy that we were
obliged to lay by, it not being safe to travel.
—From the diary of Lydia Allen Rudd, during the last weeks
of a six month journey.

WINDS OF RESISTANCE

Three years after the "visions" had started, three years after
an innocent little trip to Arizona, I sat alone close to the
Colorado/New Mexico border, heading southbound and
steeply up on Interstate 25 in a Budget rental truck. My 1990
Honda hung behind on a tow dolly, and my body and mind were
shot after having driven twenty-five hundred miles in three
days, and after having lived the three years that had preceded
those three long days.

Yet my diary entries from that day and the few that followed
barely touched on the tedious journey from the American

Dream life in a rural coastline community in New York to something else.

~~~

Friday, June 5, 1992
Raton Pass, New Mexico

"New Mexico... HOME!
Tears came to my eyes as I passed under the bright yellow and red "Welcome to New Mexico" sign. I pulled over on the top of the rest stop here at seven thousand eight hundred-foot Raton Pass. The mountain air feels sweet and clear. The view takes my breath away. Even the fatigue of packing a truck and driving it over two thousand miles were momentarily washed away in the magic of this moment.

Immediately after that blissful rest point in eternity came new reminders, new tests. I returned to the highway, and an intense headwind pushed hard against me. The truck strained to go fifty miles an hour downhill. I looked at the gas gauge: "Empty." How similar was this waking dream to the recent weeks—to the "headwind" of resistance from my mind and my family, and to the feeling of emptiness and exhaustion that haunted me.

But the tests continued. About thirty miles south of Raton Pass, I pulled into the town of Wagon Mound, New Mexico, where both of the town's two gas stations lacked diesel fuel. "Next diesel is forty-two miles south in Las Vegas," said a young attendant. Forty-two miles. The needle already touched the "E."

I headed south into the brutal defiance of that gas-robbing headwind. The needle dropped below empty. The miles crept by so slowly. Then, a realization hit me like the wind that buffeted the truck: this was a test. "Do you want gas, or God?" I heard a voice saying, reminding me of the story Harold Klemp once told.

There was not even a moment of hesitation. "I want God," I replied to my inner voice. "The truck can go ahead and run out of gas."

Then I thought of the early pioneers on the Santa Fe Trail. The trip from Raton Pass to Santa Fe took two weeks, and that was after two or three *months* on the trail from Independence, Missouri. If I ran out of gas, I could just back the Honda off the tow dolly and get some. A slight inconvenience, maybe, but certainly no catastrophe.

Even if I didn't have an extra vehicle behind me, the situation and the question brought the same answer: "I am committed to God, not comfort, not safety, not convenience." It was why I had begun that long journey in the first place. There was plenty of "gas" back in New York, but I, like so many millions of others, was choking on it and its exhaust.

The wind pushed. The rolling hills seemed immense. The truck crawled along. The gas warning light stared at me, an orange threat. "Las Vegas 10," said the road sign. The truck sputtered. Ten miles never seemed so long. Eight. Five. Then just two. I squinted and could see the exit in the distance. Las Vegas, New Mexico sat in a broad valley. Even if the engine quit now, I thought, maybe I could coast to it.

I didn't have to. I made it. And this fact, and what followed, presented another waking dream: I would—if committed to completing the journey—get past the resistance (the headwind) and the exhaustion (the empty tank). Just like the snails in Mike Avery's book.

As I pulled back on to southbound I-25, gas tank full, I noticed the speedometer arching past sixty, then sixty-five. No problem. The wind had stopped, as if it was finished when my lesson had been learned. I cruised through the paradise of Northern New Mexico and glided into Santa Fe. As the sun dropped and the sky and mountains glowed, I saw my friend Robin Ann standing in her yard, watering her roses and fruit trees. I parked the truck, shut it off, and patted the dashboard in gratitude.

Then the strongest gusts of the day blew up.

"It's the winds of change!" Robin Ann yelled over the din with wide eyes and a beaming smile.

Her smile and hug provided a warm welcome from she who had made the journey ten years before. These are the people— the pioneers ahead of the pioneers— who ease the journey for all that follow. It is what I wished to be and why I would log every day, every thought, every feeling that surrounded this journey.

I had arrived in New Mexico, a land strikingly different from New York, yet which land had somehow called me to it.

The year and a half leading up to this blustery arrival in Santa Fe had taken its toll on my physical and emotional bodies. Both felt weary from too many changes and the incessant resistance that dwarfed those last tense miles in New Mexico.

And there was more.

Saturday, June 6, 1992
Santa Fe, New Mexico

Exhaustion.
Today was filled with fear and loneliness and tears. I drove the truck down to Albuquerque in the morning. The first sight I saw was a bumper sticker that read "Enjoy your visit to New Mexico, but please don't stay." Bad sign.

After driving around Albuquerque for hours looking for a storage place and a hand truck, I finally pulled up to a storage garage.

I unloaded the truck myself, feeling hot and shaky and weak. Two strong teenage boys stood a short distance away, but since I had run out of cash, I could not hire them. After ten minutes of unpacking, I sat in the back of the truck and cried.

Albuquerque did not feel good to me that day, either. There was too much traffic and heat for me. "Maybe the critics were right all along," I thought to myself for a minute. I pushed the thought away as I unloaded the tightly packed truck one piece at a time.

A brief exhilaration filled me when the truck was finally empty and the storage unit full . . . *I did it! I made it!* I was glad there was no piano on board.

Yet even more tests would come.

~~~

Though I felt completely wiped out, I slept fretfully on Robin's futon Saturday night. Perhaps as soul I knew what was to come. Sunday morning, as I began pouring boiling water into a thermos bottle, I dropped the thermos and spilled the water on my belly. It burned to the point of a bleeding blister. The pain was intense.

Not twenty minutes later, as I reached to take something off Robin's table, I burned my wrist on a candle flame. Outside, the wind whipped and howled.

An hour later, we attended an Eck worship service. When I got back to Robin's house, I opened up an Eckankar book, *The Shariyat-Ki-Sugmad*, by Paul Twitchell, at random. Incredibly, I read:

"Love comes to one in whom the Word has stirred. It is like the rushing of the mighty winds, and the tongues of fire . . . No student is ready for the Initiation until he has undergone the trials of the cave of fire, and the water test.

. . . Thereafter, the student enters into glorious life with the Sugmad. But until then he will be blown before the wind . . . He will suffer the agonies of spirit until the burden seems too great, and all is lost."

~~~

As yucky and tough as Saturday and Sunday were, those trials of fire and water, Monday was wonderful. David Conrey, who I had met the day before at the Eckankar service, picked me up just after sunrise in his beat-up Toyota pickup truck.

He took us to the Jemez Mountains, where we hiked up through a canyon at a place called Tent Rocks. We climbed through and then steeply up out of that canyon, treading on slippery volcanic dust.

We reached the top of a high, narrow precipice and shared a cool canteen of water. Clouds passed over. A brief drizzle cooled us, then the warm sun returned. My heart pounded on the way up, and soared at the summit.

"*This* is New Mexico," David said. As he spoke, a hawk flew past us at eye level with our high perch, screeching its own welcome.

"Now I know why I moved here," I said. "Thank you."

"You're welcome," he answered. His voice rang with such warmth and sincerity as he said those simple words that the brow-beating and bumper stickers and burning of the previous days vanished in the haunting New Mexico sky.

We hiked down to his truck, then drove over miles and miles of nearly impassable (I had to get out and push at one point) mountain roads. The air was cool and moist. The pine and cedar and aspen fragrances intoxicated me.

My heart and body felt transformed by the mountains, the hike, and the company.

As if those hours in heaven were not enough, I then went to Judy Scher's office for a Network adjustment. My body— every cell— hummed in harmonic ecstasy. Beauty filled the room and sang from my heart. I laughed as I had not laughed in many months. Warm, loving smiles followed me for the rest of the day. But there was more.

That night, just as the sun dropped below the Jemez Mountains, I drove to the ski area parking lot ten thousand feet up Santa Fe Peak. The steep, winding drive exhilarated me. Then I parked the car and walked into the cool, darkening woods.

A large, flat tree stump welcomed me as I sat to sing a love song to God. There in the high mountains above my new home, I gently sang the HU.

My ears rang. Birds sang with me. Trees whispered. The half moon looked over my shoulder through the aspen. When I returned to my car, I grabbed my journal:

Has the pioneer found his home? My heart and body—without qualification—say YES! The friends, way-showers Robin Ann and David. The mountains. The air! The ever changing, living sky. The winds of change that blow love and challenge through hearts and homes. The Eck —the humming HU song that the mountains sing. The hawks and hummingbirds.

I knew I would be flying back to New York in a day, and a tinge of fear reached through the ecstasy. I closed that joyous entry with a prayer:

Dear God, please let me be love.

~~~

Mark Twain wrote that travel is fatal to prejudice. Though I arrived "home" in New Mexico, there was still more traveling to be done. At 7 A.M. on Tuesday, June 9, 1992, his words would prove true once again.

As I waited for my plane back to New York, I started a conversation with "Violet," a Navajo woman nearly old enough to be my grandmother. I told her of our move to New Mexico from New York, including the hard parts.

"Change is good for the soul," she said.

I told her of the resistance from family.

"You've got to cut apron strings," she said.

The label "old Navajo woman" had disappeared ten seconds into our talk. A stereotype shattered on the runway. There was more. She had been to Europe and Hawaii three times, and to Cairo, where she saw Anwar Sadat. She had lived in Florida, California, and Texas. She sat calmly and spoke gently. Her wisdom flowed subtly, not in know-it-all fashion. "Violet" was her name. Navajo? No. Wise Soul.

One final waking dream left me as I headed toward the passenger gate. In the center of the terminal stood a larger-than-life bronze by Santa Fe artist Lincoln Fox titled, "Dream of Flight." I thanked Twain and "Vi" and God as I read the inscription:

The dream of flight is born within the heart of man, embracing the desire to be free from the confines of the earth's surface.

Hopefully the dream includes the possibility of freedom from limiting thought and action.

As our imagination is freed to receive greater truths, then fear, closed thinking, and poverty of spirit will be left behind. . . far below.

THIRTY-FIVE

The road is worse than ever. Lou and I walked the whole ten miles, till we came to within a mile of Ragtown. We saw trees on the Carson River and thought we were almost there but we kept going and going and it seemed we would never get there.
—From the diary of Jane Gould Tortillott, September 15, 1862

THE LONG ROAD HOME

Wednesday, June 10, 1992
Southold, New York

What a world. Yesterday, I watched the sunrise over Santa Fe Peak. That same evening, I ate dinner at Pizza Hut on Long Island with Annie and Kate and Andrew.

The house I had left ten days before was no longer our home. Our TravelMaster motor home sat in my parents' driveway. I walked into their house to say hello. As soon as I had walked into his TV room, he clicked the mute button. "How was your flight" was the last small talk of that evening. Immediately, we started talking with the same angry tone of our heated exchange on moving day. The grilling that had begun nearly two years before—on that morning in my office when I told him I was leaving the law and New York—continued that night. I knew my journey had not yet ended.

Dad yelled. This time, I yelled back. I blasted his life-style as I had done for so long in my dreams. He threw out the phrases Annie and I had heard from others that year, "Maybe you're just a malcontent," and "there isn't greener grass there" among them.

Don Epstein had often spoken about a stage of healing he called "resolution through discharge." Discharge often took physical form as coughing, vomiting, or diarrhea. That night the discharge, for both my father and me, was anger. But it felt there would never be a resolution. The chasm between us remained.

Then, after several loud "But you said this!" and "But what about this," when our anger was spent, the tone suddenly changed. As midnight approached, my father stepped out of his recliner.

The discharge had made room for a bridge across the gulf. My father and I had each descended into the Grand Canyon of judgment and anger that had separated us since the day I told him I was leaving my law practice. We met at the bottom, and embraced on what felt like the way back up.

"I love you, John Michael," he said, kissing me on the cheek, hugging me with his big arms.

"I love you, Dad."

~~~

The physical road from New Mexico back to New York was like flying through the air at five hundred miles an hour while a flight attendant served lunch. *Just* like it. The drive from New

York to New Mexico, though we would travel at a slower speed, would not be much harder. But as Dad and I began our thunderous clash just hours after my touchdown in New York, I knew the two weeks leading to our departure would be trying. There were more canyons into which I would have to descend. And as each hour passed and every meeting became a sad farewell, it seemed we would never get there.

On a balmy East End June 15, we sat behind Southold School watching Katie sing and dance in her last kindergarten show. After the closing ceremonies, her wonderful teacher told us how Katie had cried in school that morning because she "doesn't want to go." My stomach knotted. I nearly cried with guilt, right there on the school grounds.

A few minutes later, her teacher told us of another little girl who had been crying for the same reason. "She didn't want to leave kindergarten, either," her teacher said.

On Tuesday, June 16, I closed my last mortgage with clients Mark and Cathy Squires. During the closing, I told them how my mother seemed to be tiring of our presence in her driveway.

"Come stay at our house," Cathy insisted. "You can park the motor home right behind our pool and use the hot tub."

Until that warm invitation, I had wished our moving day was sooner. Cathy and Mark reminded me that the "journey" was not about us moving to New Mexico, but about moving into the flow of Life.

Life's currents were carrying us over new waters.

The following day, as we sat in the Squire's yard, I felt sad that we were not with my family. That night, we (Mark, Cathy, Annie and I) sat at a down-home feast of barbecued chicken and salads and shared stories of love for animals, which led to dolphins, which led to hugging trees. That led to the Pleiades to Tanzanite to ghosts to religion to Network Chiropractic to heart/mind connection to sex to children to role models to religion to kinship to DNA frequency change.

I wrote about the wonderful gathering in my diary that night, then wrote, *Now I have an idea why we were invited here.*

On Saturday, June 19, we stopped at Florence and Jim ("Gramma and Grampa") Murray's. They had baby-sat for Kate since she was six weeks old. They had become like real grandparents to Kate and Andrew, and dear friends to Annie and me. Now it was time to say goodbye.

Florence kissed and hugged me, then walked quickly out of the room to hide her tears. *Why are tears so shameful for so many?* I wondered to myself as I stood there crying.

Jim hugged me tightly—I didn't think he would— saying "We'll miss you guys. We really will." I cried, promising we would be back at Christmas.

"I hope you are, and I hope we're here," Jim said, turning away.

Kate and Andrew said "Bye, Gramma and Grampa," just as they did every time we had picked them up at the end of the day. Oh, to live in the present moment!

Sunday, June 21, 1992
Father's Day

It's seven A.M.— birds chirp. Today our motor home is parked in front of Annie's parents' house.

Annie just put on her purple robe and walked from our mobile house into her mother and father's house. She looked pensive even as she woke up.

"I'm nervous about today," she said.

"Say a little prayer," was all I could think to say. Better to reconnect with what is real and important than for me to philosophize.

This casting off might be the toughest part of any "pioneer's journey." Imminent goodbyes to family and close friends brought emotions to a near apex.

Annie's parents were quiet as we arrived last evening. Later that night, while Annie's mother and father watched Kate and Andrew, we went to yet another goodbye.

We sat on the deck of Annie's long-time friends, Richie and Gary. Gary told us how hurt he felt when his brother had moved away five years ago. "The family will never be the same," he said. "I'll never forgive my brother."

Gary showed a side of this journey that I had denied all this time; that the world of those who stay behind is shattered by the fact of the other ones leaving. They <u>hurt</u>. The voyager's world shatters, too, but they have chosen that course more consciously.

Today we will be with Annie's mother and father and all of her family. Today I will remember their pain, whatever mask it wears. In her "little prayer" this morning, Annie asked for help in being loving and compassionate.

I feel so naive. All we did was decide to move to the Southwest, yet the changes and ripple effects are beyond what I cold have imagined. Crying, and bitterness, and worlds expanding, and worlds exploding, and deaths . . .

That day, at a Father's Day barbecue in Annie's brother Bob's backyard, the pioneers said goodbye to Annie's parents and brothers and sisters-in-law and nephews. Two days later, we would literally drive into the sunset from a Hall gathering, over the shattered glass of an older, more rigid world and into the

233

bright light and surroundings of a world changed by the simple choice of two people.

But that was two days away. More farewells beckoned.

Monday, June 22

I have lived a lifetime in these past two days.

Goodbyes expressed, and unexpected, new bonds made and accepted.

Mark and Cathy Squires, and their children Maxwell and Marak. Wonderful people. A special relationship made out of this journeying process.

But most of the what occurred during that part of the journey would have to wait. Those last forty-eight hours in Southold simply overwhelmed my ability to write.

~~~

THIRTY-SIX

Have the elder races halted?
Do they droop and end their lesson, wearied over there beyond the seas?
We take up the task eternal, and the burden and the lesson,
Pioneers! O pioneers!

All the past we leave behind,
We debouch upon a newer mightier world, varied world,
Fresh and strong the world we seize, world of labor and the march,
Pioneers! O pioneers!
—Walt Whitman, *Leave of Grass*

LAND HO!

"Land ho!" In my history book, perhaps the same one that had the picture of the homesteading family in front of their sod hut, this is practically the first image I got of Columbus's voyage. The sentry stood high in the crow's nest of the Niña shouting, "Land Ho!" The textbooks follow with a description of Columbus kissing the ground in the "New World."

The history book never mentioned the tearful good byes of the crewmens' wives, mothers and children back on the coast of Spain. Those family members thought their sailors were going to their doom, but the textbooks hardly mentioned it. They never told about the toil of each crewman sweating and straining to load and unload provisions and casks of water on and off the ship, either.

And we never read about Christopher's own doubts. Did he second-guess himself as I had? Did he anguish for months over whether or not he was crazy for wanting to sail off the edge of the flat earth? Did his family and friends talk about him behind his back? Did he look at his wife and children over and over, asking, "Should I really be doing this or should I stay safe and sound here in Spain?" None of that reached our history books. Just "Land Ho!" followed by Columbus kissing the ground.

It was the same with the Pilgrims. We all know about Plymouth Rock. As we made paper feathers and prepared out Thanksgiving feast in school, we learned that many died during the voyage from Europe and that they left because of religious persecution. But nowhere did the books or teachers they tell the story of the people the Pilgrims left behind in Europe who said "Please don't leave me." or " What are you going *there* for?"

~~~

Friday, June 26, 1992 8 P.M.
At the welcome center, New Mexico, U.S.A.

Only four days have passed since I wrote last. Now I know how illusory time is, for many lifetimes have passed.

Tuesday morning, Annie and I cried as we said goodbye to John Klindienst and Jamie and Joshua and Merienne. John and I hugged for a long time, then he suddenly ran upstairs. I never thought I would see him cry.

Tuesday afternoon, we made our final preparations, hitching up the '85 Honda to the tow dolly in back of the TravelMaster.

At four o'clock Tuesday afternoon, all the Halls gathered at Nancy and Steve's house for a farewell dinner. Mom and I hugged and started to cry as soon as she got there. After that, all of us maintained our usual cheerful, joking exteriors for as long as possible. But the time for pretending this was just a regular summer gathering and that we were not leaving had ended.

As soon as dessert was finished, they all presented us with some very special gifts, including a CB radio and an "Over the Rainbow" tape and music box. But we couldn't hold out any longer: it was time for us to go.

The tears started. First, Mom and me again. I started to feel her pain, as she embraced her youngest son, her "baby boy." Then Bobby, my tender-hearted big brother, nearly enveloped me with his embrace. "You can just pretend this is a long vacation and come back at the end of the summer," he whispered in my ear. Bob and I hugged for a long time, and cried in each other's arms.

Then Nancy, my "little" sister, who had made her own rugged pioneering journeys through life. Then Steven, and Ellen. Then Bob's children Michael, my namesake, and Briana, who was born the night I had proposed to Annie, said goodbye. It felt like a funeral, as they lines up to say their farewells. Part of us each of us died that evening. Certainly a family tradition of all living within minutes of each other had. Then Ricky came up to my coffin.

"I love you," he said, squeezing my hand and looking right through me. "I love you," he repeated with a strong tone and piercing eyes. Later, I wondered if that was Spirit, itself, talking to me through Rick.

Then Dad. Dear Dad. He tried so hard to keep smiling but could not. We cried together. Earlier that morning, during a gentle conversation, he asked me not to let pride prevent me from coming back. I didn't react hostilely that time. I hoped I would not let pride prevent me from anything. But his words did not seem to apply to this trip as some wished. Annie and I were not running away from home; we were starting something new.

Before we left Nancy's house, Nancy looked me in the eye and said, "Thank you for everything, Michael." Her words, and a love I had not seen in my family in thirty six years caught me by surprise. Love poured from each of them to all of us (even to Annie, about whom there had been mixed feelings for months). Their love that evening washed away the ill will I had carried inside for so long.

"If we <u>do</u> come back in two months, boy are you are all gonna be pissed," I said.

The laughter from my joke was short-lived; we continued our teary goodbyes as the four of us hopped into the car to drive back to the waiting motor home. My entire family came out to Nancy's driveway to watch us drive away. Annie squeezed my hand as I looked in the mirror at my family and we took our last drive away from New York, sobbing.

~~~

But that was a lifetime ago. Since that moment, we have driven two thousand miles and spent a day in rural Pennsylvania with Dad's sister, Joan and her husband, Rich.

Since that emotional moment, we've chatted on the CB radio with thoughtful truck drivers, one of whom even told me where I might find a job in Albuquerque.

So here we sit, 216 miles outside of Albuquerque. Trucks whiz by on I-40. Annie sleeps in the bunk above me. Kate and Andrew just fell asleep in the back.

As if Spirit (or the "negative" forces) had to make one last effort to hamper this move, or temper those who dared make *it, we drove into a savage, raging thunderstorm just as we approached the New Mexico border. The sky blackened. Lightning flashed all around. Rain fell like the tears of Tuesday. It fell so hard, we had to pull off the road while the storm passed.*

And, true to the Wild West, pass it did. In ten minutes, the fierce storm roared behind us, and the sun illuminated puffy, white clouds behind the storm into giant sky castles. Rainbows filled the sky as we drove west into fresh, cool blue.

"I just realized," Annie said just before we entered New Mexico, "we're not going back after this trip." I thought I saw fear in her face as she said it, then she smiled the broad, gleaming-white smile I saw the day I met her. Now she sleeps soundly, here in New Mexico.

And —and this may seem trite in the context of the emotional rains of the past weeks—I could not help but feel awe as we cruised across two-thirds of the continent at sixty-five miles an hour in air-conditioned comfort. What we covered in three days may have taken the first pioneers a year. Or did we do it in three days?

As I flipped back through my journal, I saw large hunks of our two-year odyssey. No, it had not just taken three days. No amount of modern technology can speed the journey toward freedom.

My last entry that night, as my brave family slept at the New Mexico Welcome center, was:

Well, we are here.
As Kermit the Frog once said, "We have done what we set out to do. Thanks to the lovers, the dreamers, and you."

EPILOGUE

The restlessness that propelled the emigrants across the continent did not abate when they reached the coast. They moved and moved again . . . So many roads seemed to lead to success that new beginnings became a way of life.
—Lillian Schlissel, *Women's Diaries of the Westward Journey*

THE SWALLOWS OF CAPISTRANO

I wish I could tell you that, on the day after that welcome center journal entry, we found the "perfect place" and set up house. I could not. We had not left New York to find a "reasonable facsimile" home or lifestyle in New Mexico, so such a scenario was impossible. The pioneers had arrived in a place where they did not know even what "home" was. The weeks that followed reflected that.

Our first six weeks in New Mexico saw confusion and anger in the midst of a record heat wave. The strains of living three months in limbo in an eight-foot by twenty-seven-foot box nearly brought our frazzled nerves and shaky marriage over the edge. But we kept moving. During that period, as we visited a T-shirt shop in Aspen, we saw a shirt that summed up or journey with the efficient writing of a poet: "I know when one

243

door closes, another opens," it read. "But these hallways are a bitch."

Something in me had changed in that hallway (or should I say "Hall"-way): At the end of August, I wrote not to my journal, but to the mother and father and brothers and sisters I had left behind, the ones on the other side of the grand canyon I had spent two years building:

September 2, 1992

Dear Family,

I started this letter a month ago. Much of it is dated. But . . .
Mom, thanks for your heart-touching letter. It meant a lot to me.

Nancy and Steve (and everybody else), thanks for the going away dinner. That, too, was very special.

Thank you to Rick and Ellen for the "Over the Rainbow" music and the kids' watches.

And thank you to all of you guys for the CB . . . and your love.

As I write this, I am sitting in our motor home, presently parked in the driveway of John and Judy Graham, friends we met two weeks ago and who invited us to stay here while they traveled to swim with dolphins in Florida. Their house sits in a subdivision called Eldorado at Santa Fe. It's about ten miles outside of Santa Fe. It is also where we will live for this coming year (Eldorado, not John and Judy's driveway!)

We looked at no less than thirty houses in and around Santa Fe. None were "right." Finally, Annie looked at a beautiful, four-bedroom solar here in Eldorado and loved it . . . but someone who had arrived at the house twenty minutes earlier had already taken it. So we keep looking.

From where I sit, even here at my computer in the motor home, I can see almost a hundred miles to the south, past Albuquerque, and maybe a hundred to the west. Smaller mountains fill the view to the north and east. Santa Fe lies at about seven thousand feet. From the high elevation here in Eldorado, you can see the lights of Santa Fe at night. Yet there are no street lights out here, so at night you can also see what seems like every star in the Milky Way.

Sunrises on the cool mornings here are gorgeous. The sunsets? Three hundred sixty degrees of spectacular. On any given night, the sky flashes with lightning storms that may be a hundred or more miles away. Clouds flash white and pink and orange in the distance. The other night, we saw two coyotes walking through a field.

A few nights ago, Robin Ann watched Kate and Andy while Annie and I went to a concert at the Santuario Guadaloupe in downtown Santa Fe. The Santuario was a church built by Spanish missionaries in the seventeenth century. Three-foot-thick, white-washed adobe walls reached up forty feet to hand-cut "vigas" (round beams). A huge fresco of Jesus and Mary covered the wall behind where the altar once stood.

Even though this three hundred fifty year-old building no longer served as a church, something very special happened in that place last night.

Carlos Nakai, a Native American man wearing traditional braids and a white linen shirt, spoke before he played. "What I do," he said, "is not about a tradition that is three hundred years old. Tradition is what we live and create in each present moment."

Then he blew the first, haunting notes into his wooden flute. The audience of two hundred froze in their chairs. His sounds

245

and melodies carried me beyond this world. Annie clutched my hand as we were awed at the magic. We had traveled to a sacred place . . . then entered the <u>heart</u> of it.

If half the people in that audience felt half of what I did, then one hundred souls sitting in that place, re-made sacred that night, experienced the Dance of Joy and Freedom that is their legacy from God.

During intermission, we walked outside the church and were greeted by the cool, sweet, mountain air that follows the sunsets here each evening, and a glowing New Mexico sky. It felt more like the astral plane than the physical.

Nakai was accompanied by a gentle pianist named Peter Kater. As they played together, the church roof seemed to open up to heaven. I felt Annie's hand hold mine. I whispered, "I think we're in the right place." Her broad smile and the twinkle in her eye affirmed my words.

So is the grass really greener here? Before I get to that, I need to share just one more in a series of stories worthy of a good book . . .

One night, while we were still living at the state park, we climbed the switchback road to our campsite. In a Ponderosa and Aspen forest nine thousand feet up, we were greeted by new friends Karen and Britt, who we met at the Network chiropractic office here, and Britt's sister, Carrie. A few minutes later, David Conrey arrived.

As I lit a campfire, Annie walked over to the adjoining campsites to invite our neighbors in the woods to eat with us. Kevin and Gloria and a man named Dean, a retired Wall Streeter, all joined our spontaneous mountain gathering.

Kevin and Gloria travel around the country with their black dog, Corazón (Heart) in a Honda wagon, paying for each penny of their trip by playing violin and guitar on the streets in tourist spots. They harness a little sack on their dog as they perform, as their unique way of "passing the hat."

Eleven of us sat around the campfire, feasting on fresh tortillas heated in a pan over the fire, covered with beans and cheese and lettuce and tomatoes. After dinner, Britt and Annie whipped up an incredible, unplanned Brown Betty with some fresh apricots Britt had brought from her backyard.

As dessert baked over the fire, Kevin and Gloria brought out their instruments. They played some traditional songs you might expect, "Oh Suzanna," and "Puff, the Magic Dragon." Then they played some hauntingly beautiful classical, Gaelic, and original tunes their in our high mountain home.

Before we knew it, the sky had turned from light to star-filled, and we all scrambled in the dark for our sweat shirts. The fire backlit Andrew as he danced to the music. Kate and Annie square-danced with Karen and Britt, then waltzed in the fire's glow. I took some pictures, but they will never —could never— capture the cool smell of the pine forest, the crackle of the fire, the sound of the music, or the magical feeling of that evening.

"It doesn't get any better than this." Dean said. It spooked me. They were the exact words Dad always used at moments like that. It was if he had followed me to the mountains of New Mexico and realized the beauty in what I had done.

So, is the grass any greener here, or is all of the above cow pie?

First of all (and I think I can speak for Annie here, too), these have been the hardest two months of my life. If I felt doubts over the previous several months about the idea of making this big, crazy move, the reality of getting here and the fears that followed dwarfed them. Houses are more expensive than planned. Seventeen elementary school districts needed to be chosen from. Good neighborhoods. Bad ones. "What are we doing here? Do I belong among these real artists, among these

247

*indigenous Indians and tenth-generation Hispanics, some of
whom resent the elite, Anglo invasion? Do we belong back in
Southold? Do we belong anywhere? Are we crazy?"*

*Those were just a few of the doubts and questions. Every little
doubt and fear and self-question that may have hidden in the
cracks before our move crawled out and grew in the Santa Fe
light into huge, life-threatening monsters.*

*Yet each time Annie and I looked at each other and said,
"Should we go back?" or "Should we go someplace else?" a
quick and harmonious "no" resounded between us. So we just
kept looking at houses and feeling like crap and looking at
houses. We plugged ahead.*

~~~

*We finally found a nice, new rental house and moved in on
August 10. My new life began immediately: Three days later,
before all of our boxes had been emptied, I left our new house
at dawn and drove to Arizona. There I walked in silence with
shaman Winged Wolf (Heather Hughes-Calero) through six
miles of lush, deep canyon in Sedona, Arizona. The last three
miles, the canyon was so narrow,we hiked waist-deep in the
water.*

*Three days after I returned from Sedona, I flew from Albu-
querque to Denver to Minneapolis, then drove to New Jersey
with Michael and Sharon to attend a Transformational Gate
there, as well as Michael and Sharon's wedding. I danced at
their reception until midnight, then left New Jersey at 4:00
A.M. and drove until midnight. I had gone a thousand miles. I
pulled over and slept four hours in the back of Judy Scher's
Honda outside of St. Louis, then woke up at 4:00 A.M. and
drove the breadth of Missouri, Oklahoma, and Texas.*

Just before sunset, I reached the New Mexico border. There *the flat plains of West Texas instantly gave way to red rock and green mountains and cliffs. I knew I was home. Fifty miles from our new house, I turned north in the dark off of Interstate 40 towards Santa Fe. From that distance, I could see the sky flashing over Eldorado, as it does there almost every night. As I approached Eldorado, in the mountains by our house, a huge cloud hovered overhead, glowing pink and white.*

I said good night to the glowing cloud and turned into our driveway, having driven two thousand miles in forty-one hours. Hugs and kisses from my beaming wife and children greeted me at the door.

So, crazy, loving family, to answer the question much posed in the earlier parts of this epoch, is the grass greener here?" NO. It's kind of a pale greenish/silver. The grass is definitely greener in Southold, New York . . .

But the SKY IS BIGGER AND BLUER HERE . . . and the possibilities, from this new starting point, are boundless!

I love you,

~~~

We were home. After two years of unceasing anguish, we had found a very special place where, and from which, we could continue our life journeys. The comments from folks back East continued ("What are you *doing* there?" and "Do you have a *job* yet?"), but from our new base camp in the high mesas of New Mexico, those comments seemed like cries from an old, far-off world.

We, my brave wife and children and me, had descended into and climbed out of the dark worlds of fear and doubt which have confronted every pioneer who has walked this earth. We had followed a vision, and turned a dream into real life. No greater freedom than this exists. But more treacherous canyons would confront us each time we stepped into new territory . . . or dealt with the old.

Sending that letter to my family felt like building a bridge across the canyon which had separated me from my family for most of the previous year. But I had more to learn about myself, so the bridge was frail and unstable. In the years that followed our move to New Mexico, I would live my ultimate terror: I would fall off that flimsy bridge into the depths of the great canyon. As I fell, I would contrive a thousand ways to avoid the inevitable death awaiting me at the bottom . . . then perish. I may share *this* journey in *The Walk Alone.*

On the day I had started my Medicine Walk in Sedona, I had reached the last page of the spiral notebook which had traveled with me for the previous six months. The time had come to start a new journal, and a new journey, the walk alone."

The last entry in that full notebook read:

The Swallows of Capistrano
Those swallows listen to their call without the noise and clutter of "shoulds" or "What will my mother think if I fly to California this spring?" They just do it.

As I turned from Interstate 40 last week and saw the lights above Santa Fe, I felt the call that had brought us here for no logical reason, the call that had overcome all inner and outer obstacles.

Everyone has a call. It is part of life in this universe. Most people either pretend it doesn't exist, rationalize it away, or struggle to push it out of their lives. Over the past thirty-six years, I had done all three.

But there comes a time, in one lifetime or another, that to ignore the call —to push away Spirit's song— becomes excruciatingly painful. Feelings of death and grief followed me around until Annie and I committed to move West almost three years ago.

Even after we arrived here, my mind ground and tore away at me. "What the hell are we doing here, anyway? Are we crazy?" Nag, nag, nag. We persevered, but why? Why this big, crazy move?

It doesn't matter. Our duty is to heed the call, the way the swallows do, not to analyze Spirit's purpose.

Since we have settled here, I have experienced an inner bliss and rapture beyond my wildest dreams. This place feels more like home than any place I have lived in or visited in this lifetime. Every cell in my body, every synapse in my brain, rejoices our arrival here. My eyes glow in ecstasy each time I look around. My feet sing as I walk this hard, dry earth.

When the swallows arrive in Capistrano each spring, do they question their long, dangerous journey? Do they wonder why they didn't just find a comfortable place near the equator? No. They just sing . . . and fly . . . and go on.

I shall, too.

Thank you, Spirit, for those who have walked the path ahead of me . . .

and returned to show the way.

Michael Hall is currently living in Santa Fe with Annie, Kate, and Andrew. They are still putting miles on their TravelMaster motor home. He is writing *A Beginner's Guide to Higher Consciousness*, which is scheduled for release in 1995, and living *The Walk Alone*.

Please write to Michael Hall care of Golden Heart.

Golden Heart Publications
PO Box 6759
Santa Fe, NM, 87502

You can purchase *Flight Lessons* or *Pioneer Journal* at your local bookstore or from the publisher at the above address. To order by mail, please send $10.00 plus $1.00 shipping for each book ordered.

Bookstores can obtain *Flight Lessons* (ISBN 0-9634920-2-0) or *Pioneer Journal* (ISBN 0-9634920-3-9) through New Leaf, Moving Books, or Baker & Taylor

I took this journey and wrote it for myself. If by seeing my struggles, you, the reader, see something of yourself, great. Though we may never meet, we are connected, and I relish—I dance—in your awakening. If my struggle with enlightenment touches you, your enlightenment brightens me. Your journey helps to map our universe, so that all may journey on. If you write to me (please do), or we meet, I will listen. For I honor and love the god in you.

All of the following have been important in my own journey toward waking up, a journey that never ends. If you would like more information on some of the teachings or groups mentioned in this book, write to them. Let your heart guide you, and listen closely, 'cause it *whispers.*

Eckankar, or the HU:
Eckankar,PO Box 27300, Minneapolis, MN 55427

Network Chiropractic:
Association for Network Chiropractic
444 North Main Street, Longmont, CO 80501

The Pleiades:
Bold Connections Unlimited, PO Box 6521, Raleigh, NC 27628

Pre-Cognitive Re-Education:
PO Box 994, Carmel Valley, CA, 93924

Shamanism, as taught by Heather Hughes-Calero:
The Eagle Tribe, PO Box 1797, Cottonwood, AZ 86326

Have fun!